BETTER RUNS

25 Years' Worth of Lessons for Running Faster and Farther

Joe Henderson
West Coast Editor, *Runner's World* Magazine
Editor, *Running Commentary* Newsletter

Human Kinetics

Library of Congress Cataloging-in-Publication Data

Henderson, Joe, 1943-
    Better runs : 25 years' worth of lessons for running faster and
    farther / Joe Henderson.
        p.   cm.
    Includes index.
    ISBN 0-87322-866-9
    1. Running.   2. Running--Training.   3. Running races.   I. Title.
    GV1061.H386   1996
    796.4'2--dc20   95-14571
                                                                          CIP

ISBN: 0-87322-866-9

Developmental Editor: Julie Rhoda
Assistant Editors: Susan Moore, Ed Giles, and Ann Greenseth
Editorial Assistant: Andrew T. Starr
Copyeditor: Lee Erwin
Proofreader: Pam Johnson
Indexer: Barbara E. Cohen
Typesetter and Layout Artist: Kathy Boudreau-Fuoss
Text Designer: Judy Henderson
Photo Editor: Boyd LaFoon
Cover Designer: Keith Blomberg
Photographer (cover): Chris Noble/Tony Stone Images
Printer: United Graphics

Human Kinetics books are available at special discounts for bulk purchase. Special editions or book excerpts can also be created to specification. For details, contact the Special Sales Manager at Human Kinetics.

Printed in the United States of America

10 9 8 7 6 5 4 3 2 1

Human Kinetics
P.O. Box 5076, Champaign, IL 61825-5076
1-800-747-4457

Canada: Human Kinetics, Box 24040, Windsor, ON N8Y 4Y9
1-800-465-7301 (in Canada only)

Europe: Human Kinetics, P.O. Box IW14, Leeds LS16 6TR, United Kingdom
(44) 1132 781708

Australia: Human Kinetics, 2 Ingrid Street, Clapham 5062, South Australia
(08) 371 3755

New Zealand: Human Kinetics, P.O. Box 105-231, Auckland 1
(09) 523 3462

To George Sheehan
for speaking—and living—the advice
that all runners—and writers—need to hear:
"Winning is never having to say I quit."

Contents

Foreword   ix

Acknowledgments   xi

Introduction   **Better Ideas**   xiii

PART I: PLANS AND PROGRAMS   1

Chapter 1   **Better Goals**   3
   Recovery Goal · Improvement Goal · Survival Goal

Chapter 2   **Better Choices**   11
   Winning Choice · Timing Choice · Racing Choice
   Walking Choice · Resting Choice

Chapter 3   **Better Workouts**   21
   Pleasant Work · Surprising Work · Simple Work

Chapter 4   **Better Walks**   29
   Walking Breaks · Walking Long · Walking Tall

Chapter 5   **Better Rests**   37

Earned Rest · Partial Rest · Masters Rest
Pre-Race Rest · Post-Race Rest

Chapter 6   **Better Schedules**   47

Three-Day Schedule · Rotating Schedule
Marathon Schedule

Chapter 7   **Better Results**   55

Written Results · Metric Results
Projected Results · Age-Graded Results
Record Results

PART II: RUNNING AND RACING   69

Chapter 8   **Better Paces**   71

Slower Paces · Faster Paces
Truer Paces · Record Paces

Chapter 9   **Better Distances**   81

"Junk" Distance · Minimum Distance
Honest Distance

Chapter 10   **Better Courses**   89

Street Courses · Trail Courses
Shared Courses · Out-of-Town Courses

Chapter 11   **Better Seasons**   99

Hot Seasons · Cold Seasons · Changing Seasons

Chapter 12   **Better Speeds**   107

Track Speed · Mile Speed
Minimum Speed · Racing Speed

Chapter 13   **Better Tests**   117

CBS Test · 12-Minute Test · One-Mile Test

Chapter 14 **Better Extras** 127

Extra Warm-Up · Extra Stretching · Extra Strength
Extra Biking · Extra Water

Chapter 15 **Better Tactics** 137

Taper Tactics · Warm-Up Tactics · Pacing Tactics

Chapter 16 **Better Races** 145

Humbling Races · Today's Races · Counting Races

Chapter 17 **Better Rewards** 153

Higher Rewards · Personal Rewards
Tangible Rewards · Final Rewards

PART III: HEALTHY AND HAPPY 163

Chapter 18 **Better Shoes** 165

Rotating Shoes · Modified Shoes · Used-Up Shoes

Chapter 19 **Better Products** 175

Performance Products · Leg Products
Eye Products · Reference Products

Chapter 20 **Better Diets** 185

Intolerable Diets · Low-Fat Diets
Liquid Diets · Solid Diets

Chapter 21 **Better Cures** 195

Medical Cures · Cold Cures · Rest Cures

Chapter 22 **Better Coaches** 203

Coach Bowerman · Coach Manley
Coach Salazar · Coach Connelly

Chapter 23   **Better Friends**   **213**

  *Teammate Friends · Helping Friends
  Remembering Friends*

Chapter 24   **Better Thoughts**   **221**

  *Loose Thoughts · Inspired Thoughts
  Lasting Thoughts*

Chapter 25   **Better Years**   **231**

  Lasting Years · Coming Years · Fresh Years

Index   **239**
About the Author   **247**

Foreword

Joe Henderson was a runner—and he wrote about it—even before running was "cool." Although I felt I already knew him through his writings, we actually met for the first time in 1971 at the National AAU Marathon in Eugene, Oregon. His honesty and skill at relating to runners of all abilities impressed me then and continue to impress me after working with him for two decades at clinics, camps, and other projects.

Joe was one of the first runner-writers to look beyond training schedules. He articulated the enduring quality of our sport—the essence that relaxes, inspires, and allows us time to ourselves. In the hectic 1990s, not only do we need running more than ever—but we also need the inspiration of talented writers. They don't come any better than Joe Henderson, who has headed the runner-writer list for more than a quarter of the century.

Reading *Better Runs* is like having a relaxed conversation with Joe. He presents even the most complex ideas in ways we understand. Because of his long experience and hundreds of friendships with runners, he draws from a wealth of illustrative stories. He is also humble enough to admit a mistake and revise his advice. How many writers, in any field, will do that? A theme throughout his work is that theory isn't set in stone. It takes a special person to reexamine questions, pursuing new or better solutions. If you want to preview the conventional wisdom of the future, read what Joe has to say. From his continuing work in

Runner's World and *Running Commentary*, he has sifted and molded his best advice for this book.

Joe Henderson, above all, is a friend to runners. He surveys the theories and trends for us. He appreciates the heritage of our ancient sport and nurtures the values that enrich our running experience. I highly recommend this latest of his books, *Better Runs*.

Jeff Galloway
1972 U.S. Olympian and author
of *Galloway's Book of Running*

Acknowledgments

In my college journalism classes, I tell students early in each term about a principle of this profession: If you take work from one person and claim it as your own, it's called plagiarism. But if you take it from many people—and give them credit—you call it research.

This book is the product of research. I readily and gratefully acknowledge that few of the ideas here originated with me. I've borrowed from dozens of mentors, all of whom I credit in the text for their advice and inspiration.

A few more thank-yous: To my editors Barbara Shaw, Janet Heinonen, and Cristina Negron for keeping the thoughts clear and the words straight when these pieces originally appeared in *Running Commentary* and *Runner's World*. And to Ted Miller, Julie Rhoda, Susan Moore, Ann Greenseth, and Kathy Boudreau-Fuoss at Human Kinetics for shaping the material into final form.

Better

Ideas

As I sat down to start writing this book, a letter arrived from one of the grand old men of running. Joe Kleinerman, now in his 80s, sent a photocopied page from the long-dead magazine *Long Distance Log*.

I'd written a letter and the *Log* had printed it as my first piece ever to appear in a running magazine. Looking at it from a generation away, the wording is embarrassingly rough but the sentiment still applies.

"I am 17 years old and a senior in high school," the letter began. "If it is possible, could you include a few articles about the training methods employed by such great runners as Johnny Kelley, Deacon Jones, etc., to give boys like me an idea of what it takes in training to be a good long-distance runner?"

Growing up in rural Iowa, my only connection to what passed then for the big world of running was the mailbox. I ordered every available publication, hoping to find the keys to better running.

Writers of books became my coaches-from-afar. In quick succession, I read and followed Franz Stampfl from England, Arthur Newton from South Africa, Percy Cerutty from Australia, Fred Wilt from the U.S., Ernst van Aaken from Germany, and Arthur Lydiard from New Zealand.

I liked the simple security that their training schedules gave me. But what I really loved were their stories, which told who used the programs and what successes they'd achieved.

These stories brought the recipes to life by adding the spice of human inspiration to the bland how-to information. Reading what other runners had done showed me what I might do by borrowing their practices.

Not all of them worked. But some of the best lessons that experience has to teach come in the form of failed tests. Learning what you can't or won't do is as valuable to your education as doing something right from the start.

My first technical failure in running came with the so-called "tow method." I was a high school boy then, susceptible to any scheme that might make me a better runner. An article in *Track Technique* magazine promised newfound speed from hooking a water-skier's tow rope to a car and letting the car drag you at a four-minute-mile pace.

"Weird idea," I thought, "but it just might work." It didn't. Fearing my arms would rip from their sockets, I dropped the rope on the first try and never picked it up again.

But I remained vulnerable to being jerked around by promoters of training and racing gimmicks. I've tried just about all the tricks, no matter how weird-sounding: Australian coach Percy Cerutty's raw-foods diet; world-record miler Herb Elliott's heavy weight lifting; quadruple Olympic winner Emil Zatopek's combat boots and dozens of interval quarter-miles.

I've tried multi-record holder Ron Clarke's three-a-day workouts; New Zealand coach Arthur Lydiard's 100-mile weeks; British marathoner Ron Hill's decades-long string of running without taking a day off.

These tricks all worked for them, but not for me. So I canceled the experiments early. They failed my most reliable test.

They reminded me that the best ideas aren't necessarily those used by the best-known athletes and coaches, those blessed by science, those containing the highest-tech ingredients, or even those producing the most dramatic short-term results. The best ideas are those that stand up to the test of time and stay in the runner's permanent bag of tricks.

Some of the best lessons are those you learn after you thought you knew everything. I thought I had this sport all figured out 25 years ago, when writing about it for *Runner's World* became my full-time job.

I'd already raced in national championship events and in more than half the states in the U.S., run my first marathon, and set my last significant personal record. I'd contributed articles to running magazines for several years. I'd just published my first book, titled *LSD* (which stood in this case for Long, Slow Distance).

What was left to learn? Almost everything.

- Twenty-five years ago, we runners still accepted "no pain, no gain" as the only way to train. The training pendulum was swinging from one form of overtraining to another: from too many track intervals to too much road mileage. Too many of us still got hurt as a result.

- Twenty-five years ago, most runners trained only to prepare ourselves for racing, not simply to gain or maintain fitness. We usually trained only by running, and rarely stretched or lifted. As injured runners, we usually kept running until we could run no more, rarely considering alternative activities.

- Twenty-five years ago, runners ate meat before races and drank only water (if that) during runs. We ran in heavy leather shoes, abrasive cotton shorts, and droopy sweats. We timed ourselves with watches that had hands.

The 25 chapters of this book tell of mistakes made and lessons learned since that long-ago year of 1970 when I thought I knew everything. These are time-tested answers to the timeless question, "How can I run better?"

I still ask it, though the meaning of "better" has evolved for me. In the 1960s, it simply meant running faster in my short races. But it would come to have other meanings.

Better would later mean going longer, in my marathons and beyond. And more recently, running better has meant staying healthier and enjoying it more. These days, I don't measure success by minutes and seconds on a stopwatch but by new months and years added to my career.

In keeping with the 25th-anniversary theme, the book comes in 25 chapters. Each one defines "better" in its own way and tells specifically how to improve in certain areas, ranging from setting better goals to enjoying better years.

This book is my story, tracing the long journey from young racer to graying survivor. But if it were *only* my story, it might not be worth publishing, because it would be too narrow in perspective and application.

I want you to read yourself into this story, as I've always done when reading other writers. I plan to give you some recipe-like information, but I especially hope to relay the same type of how-it-works inspiration that I've always received.

Joe Henderson
Eugene, Oregon

I

Plans and Programs

1

Better

Goals

A producer of motivational tapes for athletes asked me to comment on what makes a runner successful. "Start," he said, "by identifying the greatest runner who ever lived."

I might have answered Herb Elliott, who never lost a mile race in his career. Or Paavo Nurmi, who won more Olympic gold medals than any other distance runner. Or Grete Waitz for single-handedly improving the world marathon record by almost 10 minutes.

My choice was less obvious. I picked Johnny Kelley.

He can't match the other three runners in honors won and records set, even though Kelley won two Boston Marathons and made three Olympic teams in his youth. It wasn't what he once did that makes Kelley my choice as the greatest runner in history. It was what he *kept doing*.

Kelley enjoyed the best of both worlds—early success plus longevity. Year after year, from his 20s to his 80s, he kept coming back to run at Boston. He endured.

Successful distance running draws on many traits. Speed is a gift from our parents. Physical strength helps, as do leanness of body and efficiency of movement. Mental strength—sometimes defined as a "high pain threshold"—plays a big role, as does a strong motivation to succeed.

But no trait better defines a distance runner or is more admired by runners than endurance. This is the ability to persist, to go the distance, to come back for thousands of tomorrows.

Make continued running your number-one goal. Judge your success as a runner mainly by how long you last.

The best one-line statement ever written about distance running didn't come from a coach or an author. It came from an anonymous ad writer for the Nike shoe company, who coined the phrase "There is no finish line."

As a runner, you aren't looking for places to stop but for ways to keep going. Your greatest victory doesn't come at the end of any race but in running that never ends. Look at the forces that conspire to stop you:

- Is it an injury that you worry will become permanent?
- Is it a distance or time goal that you worry will never be met?
- Is it a goal satisfied and the worry that you'll never get excited about running again?

Upcoming sections of this chapter will tell you how to come back from trouble, how to come back for better results, and how to come back less seriously.

Recovery Goal

Mary Decker Slaney has set several world records on the track during her 25-year career. But she also has established a more dubious record—the greatest number of surgeries ever endured by a world-class athlete.

Slaney's scar count approaches 20 for her running injuries. This total puts her well ahead of Derek Clayton, who had weathered nine operations when he retired as world-record holder in the marathon. Joan Samuelson, America's fastest woman marathoner, has gone under the knife a half-dozen times.

These three extreme cases dramatize that running can be risky for all of us. This sport might not carry the same risks as skydiving, rock-climbing, or downhill skiing. But runners do get hurt easily and heal slowly.

In any one year, at least half of us will suffer an injury serious enough to change our training routine, send us to a doctor, or both. If you're one of these victims, keep some facts in mind while recuperating:

- Most of these problems would be called "minor" if they weren't so disruptive to your running. For instance, a sore spot the size of a dime on your Achilles tendon—a point of pain you barely notice the rest of the day—can cripple you as a runner. The loss of running, and the uncertainty over when or if it will return, hurts worse than the injury itself.

- Most of these problems are self-inflicted. They aren't accidents like skateboarding into a car or crashing into a linebacker. Running injuries usually result from training or racing errors: from going too far and too fast too often. This is hopeful news, because if you have inflicted this injury on yourself you also hold the power to cure it.

- Most of these problems are temporary. They will eventually heal themselves if you push the right buttons. Finding a cure means reviewing the training and racing that led to the breakdown. Then you make adjustments in distances and speeds, and especially in allowing enough rest and recovery time between the long and fast efforts.

If you're dealing with a long-term injury and asking yourself, "Will I ever be able to come back?" listen to the stories of Mary Slaney and Joan Samuelson. They have spent almost as much time practicing recovery as preparing to race.

Slaney's career has alternated between up-years and down-years. One season she has set records and won championships, and the next season she has appeared to be finished as a competitor—only to reappear at the top the year after that.

Mary has been getting hurt and coming back like this for more than two decades. We've come to admire her as much for this uncanny ability to rebound as for her immense talent.

Samuelson's career pattern has matched Slaney's. But we remember Joan best for one incredible comeback. While training for the 1984 Olympic Marathon Trial, she injured a knee so severely that running was impossible. With that race just 17 days away, she agreed to gamble on arthroscopic knee surgery. The incision had barely healed when she ran the trial—and won it, setting herself up to become the first woman Olympic Marathon gold medalist.

If Samuelson and Slaney could repeatedly overcome problems and climb back to their old levels and beyond, what's to stop you from returning to yours?

© Ken Lee

Joan Benoit Samuelson runs to win the 1984 Olympic marathon—just three months after arthroscopic knee surgery.

> Know that almost no success or failure
> is a permanent condition. Always be
> prepared to move to your next level.

Improvement Goal

Runners are never too old to improve. This isn't to say that you'll keep running better indefinitely. But if you're fairly new to running, you can improve for a long time no matter what your age is.

Dr. Joan Ullyot, a well-known running writer, has observed that a 10-year rule seems to be at work in this sport. From the time you start to race, you can expect about a decade's worth of improvement. It takes that long to become fully fit and efficient, and to learn all the tricks of racing.

Priscilla Welch appears to prove the Ullyot formula, and Carlos Lopes apparently cheated it. Welch won the overall women's title at the New York City Marathon when she was 42 years old. Lopes won his Olympic Marathon title at 37 and set a world record at 38.

Welch didn't begin running until she was almost 35 years old, so at the time she won in New York (setting a world record, that still stands, of 2:26:51 for women 40 years and older) she was only in her eighth year of racing. She ran on young legs that hadn't yet taken too much of the wear and tear that slows runners down.

Lopes's running dates back to his youth. He won an Olympic medal in his 20s, then fell into a long spell of injuries before coming back to run his best marathons in the 19th and 20th years of his career. What he proved was that the 10-year improvement clock can stop and restart later with no penalty, and that a decade isn't a fixed limit.

Coming back for more and better running, at any age, may be a matter of working harder. It certainly requires working *smarter*.

You need to mix the three ingredients that form any workable program, and combine them in the amounts that work best for you. The recipe consists of these ingredients:

1. *Long runs*—long enough to prepare you for your longest race
2. *Fast runs*—fast enough to prepare you for your fastest race
3. *Easy days*—light enough to refresh you from the long and fast runs and races

> Spend your first 10 years learning to run. Expect your racing times to improve throughout that decade.

We'll talk much more about these three elements in chapters to come. But I won't keep you waiting to see the possibilities for making breakthroughs in distance, speed, and health. Here's a quick preview:

- If you're having trouble stepping up to a longer distance by running steadily, try walking. I know the word "walk" strikes a sour note with many runners, but it's a way to double instantly the length of your longest nonstop run. Take a walking break of, say, one minute for each mile of running. (Chapter 4 explains this technique fully.)

    A group of first-time marathoners in Los Angeles uses this plan both in training and in the race. Hundreds of them start the event, and 99 percent of them finish.

- If you're having trouble breaking through to a higher speed and you do little that is fast, start speeding up with the 1-1-1 plan. Run one mile, one minute faster than normal training pace, one day a week. Warm up before the fast mile, run it for time on a track or accurately measured flat road, then cool down afterward.

    A friend of mine was once stuck at 52 minutes in her 10-kilometer races. She ran these miles four weeks in a row, made no other changes in her training, and improved to 48:30 in her next 10K.

- If you're having trouble recovering from one race to the next and you're tempted into racing too often, try spacing the races further apart. Allow at least one easy day for each mile of the race.

    During this rebuilding period, run easily. Take no long runs, no fast ones, and certainly no more racing until you've filled the quota of easy days: a total of at least a week after a 10K and a month after a marathon.

Coming back for more means coming back both prepared and rested.

Survival Goal

There are three great lies in running. The first is that there can be only one winner in any race.

We now know that isn't true. We've come to see that everyone who goes to the starting line stands a chance of winning on his or her own terms. Runners wouldn't keep coming back to races if they thought all but one of them would wind up a loser.

The second great lie states that "pain equals gain." That one is at best a half-truth.

Some uncomfortable effort is required of anyone who wants to press the limits of distance and speed. But such effort must be treated as a prescription item to be taken only in small, well-spaced doses.

Running can't hurt all the time or even most of the time. Otherwise it adds up to more and more pain until you can't or won't tolerate it any longer.

The third lie says that there is no competitive life left after the last personal record (PR) is set. Why keep running after you stop improving?

I could give you lots of reasons, from 25 years of post-PR experience, why this competitive life is as good as the former one—and in some ways better. But those can wait until later in this book. For now, I'll let the stories of two former world-record holders speak for me.

Derek Clayton could have taught in the pain-equals-gain school of thought. He trained up to 200 miles a week at his peak, mostly at near-five-minute-mile pace.

Clayton's reward was that he held the world marathon record continuously for 14 years. His penalty was frequent injuries that kept him from ever winning an Olympic medal.

On retiring from racing, Clayton said, "I can honestly admit now that I never enjoyed a single minute of my running. I'm relieved to be finished with it."

He stopped running, but not for long. He soon began to miss it. He didn't miss the 200-mile training weeks or the marathon races, but simply the daily routine of running itself.

He settled into a new routine of five-mile runs, and his whole outlook on running changed. Clayton said it went from being grinding work that he barely tolerated before to "one of the bright spots in my day now."

Derek Clayton spoke of coming back for less in training. Jack Foster talked of coming back for less at races.

Foster held the world record for master (ages 40-plus) marathoners from 1974 to 1990. By the time it fell, he had long since made peace with the watch. He was racing a minute per mile slower than he did at his fastest.

But Foster said, "Only my times have changed. All the other experiences of racing that attracted me initially are the same as they have always been, and they still appeal to me."

Foster quit comparing his times, and only compared feelings. Times change, feelings don't.

Look forward to the post-PR years as your richest phase. Take pleasure in experiencing the sport at a more relaxed pace.

Everyone's times will eventually slow, and distances may shrink. But the effort and excitement of the race can remain constant throughout your running lifetime.

Look at Johnny Kelley, my choice as the greatest runner who ever lived. He won his last Boston Marathon in 1945 and made his last Olympic team three years later, but continued to find excitement and enjoyment in racing well into the 1990s.

Your ultimate challenge is not to keep exceeding yourself. It's to keep *repeating* yourself.

Your final test as a mature runner is not to get up for the big runs you've never accomplished before. It's to get back to the little ones you've taken hundreds of times before.

Your challenge is not finishing first in a single race. It's wanting to and being able to keep coming back to run the greatest race of your life, the one you can only lose by dropping out.

Satisfy your short-term ambitions of running farther and racing faster. But make it your overriding goal to keep going, to endure, to outlast over the long haul the people you might not be able to outrun right now.

2

Better

Choices

You have to go into each day with your eyes and mind wide open. Otherwise you might miss a turn that could change your life.

These turns aren't well-marked, so you can't see them coming a long way ahead. You might not even notice how much your direction has changed until you're long past that fork in the road.

Looking back over the maze-like path of my running life, I see many turns that led to dead ends. But I also see a few birthdays of new and better eras. Five stand out as the most important turning points:

1. That April Fool's day in 1958 when I learned how to win while losing. My first one-mile race ended disastrously when I dropped out in the second lap.

I could have stopped running forever that day and missed all that was to follow. But my coach, Dean Roe, kept me from taking that wrong turn by saying that finishing, not beating everyone, was the first way to win and that finishing faster than before made winning even sweeter.

2. That August day in 1966 when I learned how to race short and fast while training long and slow. I didn't turn to the slower part of renowned coach Arthur Lydiard's program in hopes of racing better, but only to escape the pains of speedwork and to finish a marathon.

   Surprisingly, this training led to faster races at all distances. It didn't work this way just because this training was slower and longer than before, but also because this training was easier. It kept me fresher, healthier, and more ready to race than I'd been while overspeeding.

3. That series of summer days in 1968 when I learned that the best "training" for racing is racing. George Young, who made four Olympic teams, convinced me that the most specific and effective way to prepare for a race was to run one.

   I turned away from all my big efforts, both fast and long, outside of races and raced almost weekly at distances from a mile to a marathon. This combination produced my best racing season ever.

4. That March day in 1971 when I learned to run longer by stopping. I'd always equated walking with cheating. Then innovative author Tom Osler promised me that by taking brief walking breaks early and often, I could double my longest nonstop distance without doubling the stress.

   Without walks, my longest run had been 32 miles. By turning to walking, I stretched that distance to 70 miles.

5. That spring day in 1987 when I learned to run better by resting. I'd been a "streaker"—which in runner language is one who runs for years on end without missing a day.

   Then my day-to-day recovery powers began to fail. On the advice of my writer friend Jeff Galloway, I started taking turns running and resting. The most convincing argument was that the days off from running (and often with the substitution of another nonpounding activity) more than doubled the pleasure of the days when I did run.

These experiences turned my running around. Changes of direction made long ago still keep me headed the right way today. Let's take closer looks at each of these five thoughts and techniques.

Winning Choice

The hardest part of racing is getting to the starting line. So many doubts and fears conspire to keep runners off that line.

We fret about failing to go the distance, or running it too slowly, or looking bad. But the greatest of all fears is that we'll finish last.

Someone has to finish last in any race. But no one wants to wind up there.

The chance of that happening in today's road races is nil. Anyone who can run the whole way at any pace can finish before the run-walkers and pure walkers.

Besides, for all we know the race directors might hire people to bring up the rear so no one else will suffer that embarrassment. The tail-ender is a rabbit in reverse—a "turtle," you might say.

No one looked out for me this way when I started racing in the dark ages. Finishing last was a real possibility in my first mile race as a high school freshman.

To avoid that terrifying possibility, I made two rookie mistakes. The first was to put as much distance as possible between me and the backrunner on the first lap. The second mistake was dropping out as exhaustion tugged me toward the rear.

A teammate of mine, Gary Almquist, finished last that day. He acted much less embarrassed than I felt, and showed me that finishing last beat not finishing at all.

I promised myself and my coach a finish the next week, no matter how far back that might be. To spare myself the shame of dropping out again, I ignored the wild first-lap dash of the boys who feared being last. I ran my own race at a steady pace that would let me complete what I'd started.

> Take winning personally. Compete only against your own standards, which no one but you can set or raise.

My whole goal was to finish (which I did), last if necessary (which I wasn't). This plan was to become the blueprint for all of my running to follow.

Start slowly, pace steadily, finish strongly. At first, these were only ways to get through the next mile. But gradually they fit into a longer view of survival.

I'm talking, of course, about the lifelong race. The race with no finish line other than the one everyone will reach. The race you can only lose by dropping out early.

During my talks to runners, I often say, "My goal is to finish last." Half the audience takes this as a joke and waits for a punch line that never comes.

I'm serious. You couldn't choose a better long-term goal for yourself than to finish last.

Set a pace that lets you keep running after all the faster starters have burned themselves out. You don't have to run very hard or very fast to beat those who stop before their finish line—or never even get to their start.

Timing Choice

You wouldn't know it from my running times today, but I'm a fast mover. I talk fast, write fast, eat fast.

I once ran fairly fast too. That was fine for races but not so nice when all the running became rushed.

All that hurrying hurt me. I adopted slower running in 1966 to ease chronic leg pains.

The slowdown helped keep me healthy. But it helped even more to relieve an illness that had infected my running.

You wouldn't know it by looking at me, but I still carry this latent illness. Dr. Meyer Friedman has identified this condition as "hurry sickness."

In his book *Type-A Behavior and Your Heart*, Dr. Friedman defines hurry sickness as "excessive competitive drive, aggressiveness, impatience and a harrying sense of time urgency. In an attempt to save time, the Type-A man often creates deadlines for himself. He is subject to more or less continuous time pressure."

This type of runner tries to cram too many miles into too few minutes. Amby Burfoot once did that. He now edits *Runner's World*, but earlier he was America's fastest marathoner and the winner at Boston.

Burfoot says that at the time he had just left college and gone to work as a teacher, "I worried about my responsibilities constantly. When I ran, it seemed I had to run fast to save precious minutes for planning, correcting papers, etc.

"Consequently I ran quite hard, didn't enjoy it as much and found rationalizations for skipping workouts. This fear of the precious minute was obviously quite neurotic."

Hurrying the longer running can make it just as unhealthful as speedwork. And worrying about wasting precious time or missing self-set deadlines can leave you unhappy at any pace.

Arthur Lydiard, the coach from New Zealand who turned me toward longer and slower running, offered at the same time a simple cure for hurry sickness: Run by the minute, not the mile.

Run with the clock, not against it. Apart from special time-trials and races, forget about how far you run and think only about how much time you spend running.

My time-running would have been worthwhile for its practical benefits alone. It eliminated the time-consuming job of designing and measuring courses, and the need to follow those routes step by step.

I was free to alter old paths and explore new ones while filling the allotted time. Minutes passed at the same rate wherever I ran them, and an accurate measurement of how much I'd run was there on my wrist.

Run by the minute, not by the mile. Make friends with the watch, cooperating instead of competing with time.

The bigger reward from time-running was slower to reveal itself. Switching to the time standard eliminated the urge to race the training runs.

The natural tendency of a type-A runner going a fixed distance is to finish it as quickly as possible, which often means pushing the pace too hard. But you can't make a period of time pass any faster.

In fact, time seems to drag when you try to rush. So your natural tendency when running for a time period is to let it pass at the most comfortable rate. You use the time to escape time's tyranny.

Racing Choice

Time is the greatest of all editors. It chooses to highlight the good memories and to scratch out the bad.

Why else would we now be seeing war babies and postwar boomers wallowing in nostalgia over 1968? When you look back on what really happened then, it was a rather dreadful year.

The country was fighting a war that no one liked and no one would win. The kids were staging a revolution of their own at home against the values of their elders. Two of the few leaders admired by youth were murdered.

I was a reluctant soldier back then who'd made a Dan Quayle-like choice to join the Army Reserve. I was training weekends under the constant threat of being called up for one of the wars, foreign or domestic.

Time hasn't yet edited out all of those bad memories, so I'm sitting out the celebration of 1968. But I can still look back on that year as my best ever in racing.

This isn't nostalgia speaking. One of the nice features of running is that its numbers resist editing. Times and distances speak the truth no matter how old they grow.

Writing about them half a lifetime later gives me pleasure. But again this isn't a purely nostalgic exercise. The lessons I learned from 1968 might still help some runners now.

I didn't plan on that year being so good and didn't see then why it was. I just got lucky and stumbled into the right combination of hard and easy, fast and slow, long and short running at the right time in my

© Photo Run/Takashi Ito

Run races frequently but allow your body to recover between them. Compete against your own standards which only you can set or raise.

life. Not knowing what I'd done right, I soon stumbled away from this mix—never to return to 1968's peak.

I ran 20 races that year. Seven of them resulted in permanent PRs, most of the others were near-misses, and there were no negative results in the form of injuries.

Only 20-20 hindsight showed me why this had happened—and why it ended abruptly. That year featured my only perfect blend of man and method.

I was 25 years old—a prime age for runners—and still not deeply into family and career duties that would conflict with running goals. This was also my 10th year as a racer, at the end of the improvement cycle that experts such as Dr. Joan Ullyot promise us.

My training was purely LSD (long, slow distance)—but it wasn't *too* long or slow. The longest runs averaged only about two hours, and most of the others ended well short of an hour.

This wasn't so much a training method as a method of *recovery* between races. Frequent racing, plus going into the races fresh and healthy, made this system work.

I averaged almost a race a week during a seven-month period. Yet most of the races were short (many were one, two, or three miles on the track), and they accounted for less than one-tenth of my total mileage that year.

The magical spell ended in a drift toward longer long runs, fewer easy runs, more long races, less track racing, and a higher overall percentage of racing. This combination led to more injuries and fewer PRs—and finally to career-altering foot surgery in 1972.

By the time I figured out what had gone right in 1968, my chance to reclaim that magic had passed. I now offer the experience to runners who still have time on their 10-year improvement clock.

Walking Choice

If "training" means going to abnormal lengths, and you like normal running too much to change it in any way, can you still finish a marathon? My experience says you can—if you're willing to try the Trick in the race.

The Trick is to take a walking break every few miles. And it's an idea that runners are slow to buy.

Maybe you're a reluctant customer who would never think of walking. To walk means you can't run—either because you're injured, you're out of shape, or you've hit a wall. Walking is for wimps.

I used to say all this too. Then Tom Osler taught me another of my most valuable lessons. He said that splitting up long runs with short walks would greatly increase their length but not add to their toll.

> Mix brief walking breaks into your runs—as a way to make long runs longer and to recover from them more quickly.

Osler first tested this method on himself in races lasting as long as two days, then wrote about it in his *Serious Runner's Handbook.* "Anyone can double the length of his or her current longest nonstop run by inserting brief walking breaks early and often," said Osler.

"Brief" means about one or two minutes. "Often" means every mile or two. "Early" means starting with the first mile or two.

Using the Trick in a race doesn't require any rehearsal in training. What it does demand is a base of uninterrupted long runs—not superlong, but about half the race distance.

My first test of Osler's advice was the most stern. The distance was 100 miles, and my longest previous nonstop run—actually a race—had been only 32 miles.

I failed the test in one way, by dropping out at 70 miles, but succeeded in other ways: more than doubling my longest nonstop distance; averaging only a half-minute per mile slower than usual marathon pace for the running portion; and suffering fewer aftereffects than if it had been a marathon.

Tom Osler had won a convert. I've since inserted planned walking into most of my marathons, and it has worked every time. The running distance gained more than makes up for the walking time lost.

Resting Choice

Before learning my best lessons from running, I had to work past some four-letter words. The curses of "lose," "slow," "fast," "walk," and "rest" all had to lift.

The last of these words, "rest," was the slowest to turn from a curse into a blessing. Only since 1987 have I acknowledged that the best thing to do some days is nothing.

Before that year, I was a streaker. I'd run as many as 1,400 days in a row.

The only way I could keep running every day without getting hurt or exhausted was to run very little each day. The amount had eroded from a late-1960s high of an hour a day to a mere half-hour by the late '80s. I was literally half the runner I used to be, and figuratively even less.

Running had gone flat. I could run a half-hour in my sleep, and almost did most mornings. This wasn't long enough to wake or warm me up.

Rarely was running ever long enough, fast enough, or tough enough to excite me, either. It held few risks, but also few of its old rewards.

Looking for more from my runs, I more than doubled their length in 1987. And knowing I couldn't do this much daily, I finally started taking the advice of George Sheehan, Stan James, and Jeff Galloway.

Sheehan, the most-read running writer, had dropped from running five to seven days a week down to three. His racing had improved at distances up to the marathon, even though he now ran only two 10-milers and a race each week.

James, one of the country's best-known sports doctors, endorsed such a plan. "I think three good-quality workouts a week can maintain a very high fitness level," he said.

"Too many people's 'quality' days aren't all that high-quality, because they're a little bit tired. Their so-called 'easy' days are too hard. We might be better off staying in bed on the easy days."

Get your rest. Value it as an equal partner to long runs and fast runs in the three-part running puzzle.

Galloway, an ex-Olympian, was my final convincer. He had decided that big *days* counted for more than big weeks. He now trained longer or faster than before on some days, but rested on others.

Galloway wrote a column titled "Those Killer Junk Miles." He described a marathoner who, "in her zeal to get better conditioning, did not take any days off. On the days that were supposed to be devoid of running, she would sneak in two to four miles.

"There was no conditioning effect gained from these runs. But by running them, she was interfering with an important process: rebuilding."

This woman had hoped to run a 3:30 marathon but only did 3:58. On her next try, she rested properly, avoided chronic fatigue, and ran 3:28.

"Our bodies are programmed to repair destruction and rebuild stronger than before," wrote Galloway. "However, this will only happen if we give ourselves enough rest.

"As we get older, our need for time off increases. Most of the over-40 runners I've worked with improved when I ordered them to run every other day."

The only improvement I sought in my mid-40s was a better feeling about the running. I wanted to leave the flatness of everyday short runs behind and to climb some higher peaks, which meant placing valleys of rest in between.

3

Better

Workouts

My best literary critic sits across the breakfast table from me. Barbara can see through my writing better than any other reader because she knows me better and is a writer herself.

After reading a column of mine, she said, "I just noticed something. You always seem to be looking for ways to make running easier."

I argued meekly, "You're not quite right. What I'm really trying to do is keep people from running *too hard*."

She wasn't finished with her critique. "I don't think most runners want to hear anything at all about running easily," she said. "They want to put more effort into their running, not less. They're trying to run as hard as they can. You risk losing them if you keep harping on the 'easy' theme."

She pointed to a letter from a reader of mine, Richard Englehart. He told of hobbling through his workouts while pushing a shopping cart to take pressure off an injured knee.

Englehart complained that "fanaticism has disappeared from our sport." He said conservative advice such as mine breeds "practical, coachable runners who are careful to avoid injury and take days off."

Barbara doesn't run much. But she knows runners well after sitting across the breakfast table from one as he moved away from ease.

Before we got together in 1987, my running had grown too easy. My average daily run had slipped in the '80s to half its old length.

I'd dropped from racing a dozen times each year to only three or four. I'd considered myself retired from marathoning, and rarely even ventured half that distance anymore.

Most of my runs had become short, slow, flat, and unbearably easy. I wouldn't say that running had grown boring, but it had definitely lost the hard edge that had made it challenging and exciting.

Guard against your routine going flat.
Fight the temptation to run the same
way every day.

Barbara's comment about "looking for ways to make running easier" might be true of what she reads from me. But she sees that advice conflicting with the changes I've made in the past few years:

- 1987 brought an apparent easing when this old streaker began taking days off. This was a tradeoff, though, to make the running days longer and harder.
- 1988 brought me back to speed in the form of weekly mile races. These were my first regular and formal visits to the track in almost 20 years.
- 1989 brought me back to the marathon for the first time in nine years. My training distances jumped accordingly.
- 1990 brought a new pattern of training that ran by three- to five-day cycles instead of weeks. Each cycle ended with a longer-than-normal run.
- 1991 brought speedwork into these cycles. This was my first training for speed since leaving college in the mid-'60s.

- 1992 brought my first two-marathon year since '72. The long training runs needed for marathons became routine again.

- 1993 brought new three-day training cycles. These allowed longer long runs, more fast runs, and frequent rest days (which served my purposes better than an easy run).

- 1994 brought monthly two-hour runs. These left me minimally prepared for a marathon at any time, without having to adopt any special training program.

This trend reminds me of a scene from the movie *A League of Their Own*. The Geena Davis character complained to the Tom Hanks character about how hard he worked the women baseball players.

"Hard?" Hanks said. "It's supposed to be hard. If it wasn't hard, everyone would do it. Hard is what makes it good."

He's right about baseball. My wife Barbara is right about running.

Runners who don't want to be like everyone else are looking for ways to make this sport harder, not easier. Easy running might keep them healthier, but hard running makes them happier.

Pleasant Work

"I don't train, never have. I don't think of running as 'training.' I just go out and run each day, and let the racing take care of itself."

Jack Foster made this comment. The New Zealander once ran well enough day by day so that a 2:11:19 marathon resulted. That time stood as a world masters best for 16 years.

Foster, now in his 60s, is the most sensible successful runner I've ever met. His approach can be traced back to the stage of his life when he began running.

He was 32 years old then and had four children to raise. Running could never be more than his hobby.

Foster wrote of his start in his autobiography, *Tale of the Ancient Marathoner*. "I was getting a little thicker around the waist. One day, I had the bright idea that I'd have a run."

When he returned a short while later, his wife asked, "What's wrong, have you forgotten something? You've only been gone about seven minutes."

"Impossible!" Jack countered. "I'm sure I ran at least six or seven *miles*." His wife's watch was correct.

He recalls, "I began running only every second day, and I was working to maintain that 20-minute jog even on alternate days. But I kept at it and began to enjoy the run itself instead of only in retrospect."

This early experience permanently shaped Foster's view of running. He refused to tolerate unpleasant training in hopes that it would pay off later as better racing. It had to be enjoyable in the doing, or he wouldn't do it.

"A reporter once asked me about the training I did," wrote Foster the year he ran the 2:11 marathon at age 41. "I told him I didn't train.

"The word 'training' conjures up in my mind sessions in a gymnasium, or grinding out 200- and 400-meter intervals. I refuse to do this."

He also didn't run "the 150 miles a week that some of the top men are doing. I rarely did more than half that. I believe it is possible to achieve results in a less soul-destroying way."

In his peak years, Foster did plenty of running. He couldn't have raced as well as he did without hard work. But it was the type of work he preferred—rather brief but fast runs over hilly sheep pastures—and not the training that experts said he should do.

> Put some challenge into your running.
> Nudge up the length of your long runs
> and the pace of your fast ones.

He said the fast racing (including a 28:46 10K at 40) came as a by-product of his outlook on running. He ran because he liked it, and by continuing to run he became very good at it—yet would have run the same way even if his racing hadn't taken him as far as it did.

"Most of my running is pleasure running," he wrote in the *Ancient Marathoner*. "The success I've had from it has been almost accidental, not planned."

In Foster's view, "It has to be a pleasure to go for a run, looked forward to while I'm at work. Otherwise no dice.

"This fact, that I'm not prepared to let running be anything but one of the pleasures of my life, may be the reason why I fail by just so much to win major races."

Without training, and by letting the racing take care of itself, Jack Foster merely took the silver medal at the Commonwealth Games the day he ran his 2:11 marathon.

Surprising Work

Runners rarely retire. They just move on to the next and more relaxed phase of their running life.

Most of the greats of the 1980s are gone or going from highest-level racing. The three Ss—Salazar, Slaney, and Samuelson—hogged the headlines throughout the decade.

But for all those three did, none of them went out holding a world best at a commonly run distance. The only American who claimed one when he stepped down was Mark Nenow in the road 10K.

His 27:22 lasted almost 10 years. He also held the American track 10,000 record of 27:20.56 for more than a decade.

Mark Nenow ran better workouts by simply doing and enjoying them.

Nenow left the top ranks of the sport at age 33, though he continued to race well at a slightly lower level. We can all still use him as a model for simplifying our running.

I met Nenow at a running seminar in Houston shortly after he'd set his world road best. He spoke without notes and answered questions with lots of "I don't knows." But his nonanswers had much to say.

Nenow didn't know his weight and resting pulse. He didn't want his blood tested or his muscles biopsied. He didn't use a computer to determine his training schedule.

He didn't remember his times from recent races. He didn't keep such records in a diary.

He said he entered competition with only the most general plan: "Stick my nose in it and run with the leaders as long as I can. That way, I either make a breakthrough or die like a dog."

Nenow was a refreshing throwback to a low-tech era. He certainly worked hard, running the high mileage at the fast pace needed to compete at his level.

But the way Nenow approached that work separated him from his contemporaries. He concerned himself only with the generalities of training steadily and racing hard, and let the specifics take care of themselves.

Such looseness required great faith that the instincts guiding him were the proper ones. Nenow trusted himself to do the right things without help from a team of coaches and scientists, and without the backing of elaborate plans and logbooks.

Balance the longer long runs and the faster fast runs with easier easy days. Follow more with less.

His way doesn't always work. He never peaked at the right time to make an Olympic team.

Yet he recovered quickly from disappointment. Failures are less devastating when expectations aren't excessive, and successes are all the more satisfying when they aren't planned.

Nenow said that all of his big improvements came as "surprises." Because he didn't set time goals, he set no artificial limits on himself.

He once passed the midpoint of a 10,000-meter race faster than his 5,000 personal record. More number-conscious runners might have thought, "Uh-oh, I can't keep going at this pace. Better slow down."

Nenow kept going, willing to risk "dying like a dog." He didn't die but improved his 10,000 time by nearly a minute.

In his late-prime years, Mark enlisted a coach and began training more traditionally. He listened to advisers who said that the marathon would be his best event, tried two, ran into injuries, and never quite reached his old standards again.

At his best, he may have been short on knowledge of running theory and statistics, but he was long on wisdom. Anyone with a little know-how can complicate something simple, but only the wise can simplify something complicated.

Mark Nenow's lesson to us all is not to let the planning and analyzing get in the way of the doing and enjoying.

Keep your running plans loose. Leave room for on-the-spot innovations that can lead to surprising results.

Simple Work

Blackberries grow wild in my home state of Oregon. The vines snake out so quickly and so far that they'd swallow up driveways, compact cars, lawns, and small pets if allowed to take their natural course. Armed with pruning shears and hoe, I battle these fruit-bearing weeds from early spring through late fall.

I need to direct the same degree of vigilance toward my running routine, which is never far from a rut. I've heard "rut" defined as "a coffin with the ends removed." The self-imposed rules of running spread like watered, fertilized blackberry vines for a practicing compulsive like me.

They wrap me in a trap of my own making. They lead to a regular, predictable sameness in the running, which stifles spontaneity, extinguishes experimentation, and smothers the element of surprise.

Looking to escape such a rut, I tried one winter to rewrite my rules. I spent most of a month's diary pages hacking away at this tangled web.

The jungle seemed impenetrable. My diary overflowed with words and numbers that groped at solutions, but none solved the problem.

I wrote of little else for an entire month, which seems a wasteful way to spend my thoughts and pages. But all this flailing served a purpose.

It led to a simple answer. It came to me in a minute after I'd searched for relief for weeks.

That morning, as often happens when I'm wrestling with a tricky idea, I started waking up an hour before getting up. Thoughts move faster than I do in that hour, and I lie back to collect them.

This one was worth losing sleep over. It cut through all my confusion.

It told me that I was too ruled by rules. I needed fewer of them, not more of the same.

One rule would do. One I could say in a single breath. One I could write on a three-by-five card and have room left over for a grocery list.

This single rule contained just numbers. The first assured against growing too lazy by asking for a certain minimum quota of running. The second guarded against going crazy by setting a maximum amount.

The numbers were "one" and "two." They stood for hours.

Run one to two hours in as few or as many days as that takes.

That's it—the entire plan in one sentence. All the rest is commentary.

Run the whole two hours in a single day (as happens only about once a month). Or take most of a week to cover as little as one hour (as happens while recovering from major overindulgences).

Let instinct and experience tell you exactly what to do each day. Decide it in the moment, not in advance. Play it by feel and by ear, not by schedule.

Run all that time. Run-walk it. Run none of it.

Run fast. Run slow. Run both.

Run steadily. Run fartlek. Run intervals.

Run the roads. Run the track. Run the country.

Run morning. Run midday. Run night.

Run hilly. Run flat. Run a mix.

Run alone. Run with a group. Run in a crowd.

This plan solved an old problem. Before, I'd traded old rules for new, one for one. Now I weeded out the old and unnecessary, clearing the training ground of obstructions and entanglements.

4

Better

Walks

He's the other Bob Anderson. Not the Anderson from California who founded *Runner's World* and is now out of running, but "Stretch" Anderson, from Colorado, who's still very much in it.

Bob II appears each summer at Jeff Galloway's running camp. While teaching stretching, Anderson was asked one year, "If someone were to do just one exercise, which would you recommend?"

Bob had a ready answer: "The Saigon squat. Asians sit in this full-squat position for long periods of time, and it stretches out most of the leg muscles. It's the single best exercise that a runner can do."

His answer raised a question of my own: How would I single out the one addition to running that has helped me the most?

I wouldn't name any stretching or strengthening exercise. Though I practice several of each, the benefits are at best subtle.

I wouldn't vote for any of today's favored cross-training activities, either: running in water, swimming, or biking. I haven't practiced any of them thoroughly enough to know how well they work.

My clear choice would be the humble act of walking. My biggest breakthrough in the past 25 years has been learning to walk again.

Walk for a few minutes to start the warm-up period before your runs. Walk again to cool down afterward.

You may not be ready to believe that it works. I too sometimes forget the value of walking in the rush to get on with running. But walking never fails to help if I give it a chance.

We aren't talking here about *race* walking, which is a demanding sport in its own right. Mine are normal walks used to fill gaps between runs.

This walking is something to do in the rest phase of interval training. Intermittent running probably is the most natural way to train (witness the go-stop-go activity of kids and puppies), and the uses of intervals reach far beyond speedwork on the track. Let me praise some of those applications:

- *Walk as a warm-up before and cool-down after running.* It's better than stretching for working out pre-run kinks. The stiffer you are, the longer you need to walk before starting to run. Walking also works better than any other exercise to ease away post-run effects. The harder you run, the more you need to walk afterward.

- *Walk to make the running faster and longer.* The interval system works both ways. By breaking a piece of work into smaller pieces, you can run each piece at a higher speed or add more pieces—without increasing total effort. Training can range from Jack Daniels's "cruise intervals" on the track (run a lap at 10K race pace, walk a minute and repeat) to Jeff Galloway's marathon plan on the road (walk a minute for each kilometer or mile of the longest runs).

- *Walk to make the running easier and safer.* For injury recovery, start by walking, and later mix brief runs into the walk, then brief walks into the run. For injury prevention, walk the steepest hills or roughest terrain. If you feel minor twinges in mid-run, walk through them to prevent any escalation in their seriousness.

- *Walk as an alternative or addition to running.* It's a satisfying form of cross-training. It doesn't mimic the physical benefits as well as some other alternatives. But walking is unmatched in mimicking the experience of running. It puts you on the same ground, in the same clothes and shoes, at the same time. These are all pluses if you need days away from running but still want to stay close to it. Walking is as close as you'll get.

Walking doesn't promise to make you a better runner any more than Bob Anderson's "Saigon squat" does. But well-placed walks will let you do more of the running that can make you a better runner.

Walking Breaks

This book runs about 75,000 words. I couldn't have sat down and blasted through all these words in one ultramarathon session of writing. Even to write a single 3,000-word chapter in one sitting would have been a dreaded, exhausting job that I wouldn't have wanted to repeat month after month.

Instead I split the book into 125 sessions of a few pages and a few hundred words each, spread across several months. None of the pieces scared or exhausted me, but the book came out on schedule.

The point here is that all big jobs go more easily if you split them up into smaller segments. This is interval training in its broadest sense.

I once took the narrowest view of intervals. They meant only speedwork and suffering, and I hated and feared them for that.

Intervals were 60-second dashes around a track, with the briefest of jogs (not walks, never rests) in between. They were repeated for what seemed like most of an afternoon, then again the next day.

They hurt me badly, both in the effort sense and the injury sense. I escaped this style of intervals forever in the 1960s.

Only much later did the late German coach Ernst van Aaken convince me that intervals at their best are the opposite of torture. They are a way to make the fast runs faster without destroying yourself, and the long runs longer without exhausting yourself.

Intervals, said Dr. van Aaken, aren't just hard speedwork. They're a basic operating principle of training. You make any big chunk of work more manageable by breaking it into smaller pieces.

I didn't buy van Aaken's argument all at once. But I've drifted further and further into his camp over the years, until most of my runs now follow the interval format.

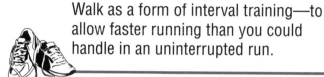

Walk as a form of interval training—to allow faster running than you could handle in an uninterrupted run.

My natural interval is one to two miles (or 10 to 20 minutes in the time-running that I prefer). The first such segment is always a warm-up, after which I walk a minute or two and decide what to do next.

The body signals say, "Go longer," "Go faster," or "Stop." I can't trust my body to tell the truth about these things until I've warmed up.

If the signal reads "Stop," this becomes an easy day. It ends with the single warm-up segment lasting only 10 minutes or so.

But if the signal says "Go," I can go either of two ways—faster or longer. The faster run typically lasts a mile, after which I walk briefly and take another 10 to 20 minutes of cool-down.

© CLEO Photography

Never underestimate short walking breaks as a way to increase the length of a run.

Other days, I run longer. The warm-up leads to another segment at a similar pace, another pause, and another decision on continuing.

These intervals can take me all the way to a marathon. This may not sound far to you, but it's far beyond the limited realm where I normally run.

The thought of running 26.2 miles would fill me with dread (and probably scare me away from even trying to run it). The act of doing it would exhaust or injure me long before the race ended (and probably in the training leading up to it).

Dread, exhaustion, and injury kept me out of marathons for almost 10 years. But treating the distance as a series of run-walk intervals has made marathoning possible again.

The marathon isn't 26.2 miles anymore. It's a long set of short intervals, from one aid station to the next.

> Walk an average of about one minute for each mile of running, taking your breaks early and often.

Walking Long

The logo on his T-shirt should have warned me even if the look on his face hadn't done so already. The face wore frown-lines of disagreement as he put up his hand after my talk. The shirt read "Western States 100."

I missed both signals while motioning for him to speak out. We'd come to my favorite part of these programs, the questions-and-comments portion, when I get to talk *with* these runners and not just *at* them.

These clinics aren't "Meet the Press." The questioning isn't usually a cross-examination, and the comments are rarely confrontational.

So I expected no strong dissent after finishing my spiel about trends in marathon training . . . about the near-perfect record of finishes by graduates of various organized training programs . . . about minimal mileage . . . about walking some if that's what it takes to finish . . . about the average marathon times now being an hour slower than they were a decade earlier.

These points—all of which were facts, not opinions—stirred the man in the Western States T-shirt. He said, "My question is, When is a marathon not a *real* marathon?" He gave his own answer.

"In my book, it doesn't really count if you plan to walk and you take all day to finish. I think there should be a stiffer qualification for counting as a real marathoner than the one you allow. You might as well count people who use bikes, or roller-skate, or hitch rides in cars."

His frown and the vehemence of his argument left me fumbling for a suitable reply. With the luxury of editing, it now reads: "In my book, if you finish a marathon under your own power it counts."

You see, the marathon isn't like any shorter race. The 10K is a race in which the question for most runners isn't "Can I go the distance?" but "How fast?"

For most of its runners, on the other hand, the marathon is a survival test. They survive the distance any way they can and take as long a time as necessary.

However, there are qualifications here:

- First, even the slowest marathoners should be trained well enough to run much more than they walk. Walks are intended only as brief, interval-style rest breathers. A marathon is, after all, still mainly a *running* event.

- Second, race officials have the right to set reasonable time limits for finishing so the roads won't stay closed and the aid stations open all day. But four hours would be terribly unreasonable, considering that the majority of any field takes longer to finish.

Four hours used to be the cutoff time for an official finish at many marathons. Now the biggest events have more finishers over that time than under.

Walk to double the length of your longest nonstop run—without a corresponding doubling of effort.

Grandma's Marathon once shut off its watches at four hours. It now lets them run for six hours, which averages out to a generous 13:45-mile pace.

I advised Ultraman to embrace the people who take hours longer than he does to finish. They are the future of marathoning at a time when the number of runners like him has shrunk too much to sustain quality events.

In this country, size and success are synonymous. The successful events attract sponsor dollars and media interest, which in turn draw even more runners.

Ultraman said he planned to run all the marathons that *Runner's World* named as the year's top 20 in the country. He would be surrounded there and vastly outnumbered by the marathoners he'd call less than "real." Their running the distance in their way makes it possible for him to run it in his.

Walking Tall

I claim no credit for the stories that follow. Each of the four quoted people drew his or her own conclusions independently, long before articles in praise of walking breaks for runners began popping up in my writing. Their response shows how far this simplest of techniques has spread.

The four testimonials tell of a varied group—a young ultraman, a short-distance runner in his mid-50s, a marathoner in his late 60s, and an ultrawoman. They used walking in quite different ways—as respites in extra-long races, as regular breaks during daily runs, and as true racewalk training.

- Kevin Setnes won the national 24-hour-run title while boosting his PR from 125 miles to 160.4. He alternated 25-minute runs with 5-minute walks after figuring that this pattern would let him run at normal training pace instead of one slower than he was used to running.

  Ultrarunning magazine writer Karl King said that Setnes's 25-5 formula has the support of researchers Tim Noakes and David Costill. Dr. Noakes notes in *Lore of Running* that runners use aerobic energy most efficiently for periods of 10 to 30 minutes. Dr. Costill says in his book *Inside Running* that walking breaks need to last at least four minutes to give the desired recovery.

- Dr. Alex Ratelle would disagree with Costill's advice. A 2:30 marathoner in his 50s, he now runs about an hour slower at 69.

  The *Minneapolis Star Tribune* reported that Ratelle inserts six to eight short walks into his half-marathon training runs, and even a few of these breaks into shorter runs. This has been his practice for 20 years.

"I walk anywhere from 20 seconds to a minute," he told writer Gordon Slovut. "You unload lactic acid and carbon dioxide during the walks. You give your liver a chance to get rid of the lactate, [which] is why your muscles are uncomfortable."

- James McFadden wrote with yet another twist on this theme. He competes as both a runner and a racewalker in the Tulsa area. At 55, he ran 5K in 18 minutes and walked the same distance in 25.

  "In almost 40 years in the sport," said McFadden, "I've never had a serious running injury. One reason is the walking.

  "I sometimes racewalk during running training, and I do days of racewalking between days of running training. I don't feel walking makes one less of a runner or a slower runner. Racewalking is my cross-training and my flexibility training."

  McFadden's practices still confound his fellow runners. He recalled training on the same track as two rivals, they running their 400-meter intervals while he walked his. A week later, he beat these same men in a 5K road run.

  "Actually walking is very hard training if you walk fast," he said. "But it is less stressful on the feet and legs. I never lose any run-ning fitness on the weeks I take off to work on racewalking events."

- Cheryl Chadwick planned to "run at an eight-minute pace for 10 miles, then walk five minutes" at a mountain 50-mile race in Montana called LeGrizz. "I would have done that, too, except that I ran too fast for the first two 10-mile blocks—around 7:30 miles. I walked a little longer to get back on schedule, but would have been better off to have run slower in the first place."

  She wrote that "the walking breaks really worked well. Just as my legs got tight, I walked a few minutes and this completely refreshed my legs."

  Chadwick won the women's race in a little less than seven and a half hours. (That's a sub-9:00-mile pace, including the walking.) She beat the women who'd won LeGrizz for 12 straight years.

  Chadwick's performance vouched for the first two benefits of walking—covering a great distance and at a better-than-expected running pace. She wrote about a third benefit—feeling better afterward.

  "After the race, I went for a hike while waiting for the awards ceremony," she said. "Again this loosened up my legs."

  The day's work had exhausted her pit crew. So Cheryl let those friends sleep while she and another ultrarunner shared the driving home.

5

Better

Rests

Each new detail of this story from my talk at the Portland Marathon Clinic caused the woman on the front row to swing her head in a wider arc of disagreement. She finally said to her partner, loudly enough for me to hear, "That's sick."

The story told of Ron Hill's running streak. He hasn't missed a day's run in 30 years. Hill had once submitted to foot surgery, but not before running that day and not without hobbling a mile—on crutches—in 23 minutes the next day.

The worst runs are the most dramatic ones in the life of a streaker. They're the ones that call the mind-set of streakers into question.

Mark Covert has known many such days, and has fielded plenty of comments that he's "sick." Covert has gone more than 25 years without taking a day off from running.

Like Hill, a sub-2:10 marathoner and Boston winner, Covert once was a racer of some note. He finished seventh in the 1972 Olympic Marathon Trial. Covert has averaged 11 miles a day during his streak, Hill 12.

"When I was younger and racing a lot," Covert told the *Los Angeles Times* on the 25th anniversary of his streak, "my attitude was that no one was going to out-tough me or out-strength me. They might beat me, but they were going to have to run hard that day. The streak was part of that attitude."

Covert now coaches track at Antelope Valley College in California. He recalled to local reporter Mike Butwell, "I got to 100 days without even knowing it. I thought, 'Wouldn't it be something to run a year.'

"A year became two, and two years grew to five. Now [the streak] has a life of its own."

Covert has fought hard to keep the streak alive. "At this point, it's a big deal to me," he said. "I don't know what it means to other people, other than they think Covert is a little wacko."

How wacko? You be the judge.

In 1980, he ran on the pitching deck of a cruise ship caught in a Caribbean storm. "The crew was taking bets on when he was going to go overboard," recalled his wife Debi.

That same year, Mark was hospitalized with a severe case of flu. When a doctor told him he must stay overnight, he says, "I popped right up and said, 'Get me out of here!' "

In 1982, Covert ran on a broken foot, suffered in a mid-run leap to avoid stepping on a snake. "I taped up the foot with an Ace bandage and [wore] a heavy construction boot, and shuffled three miles in 25 or 26 minutes. But I got my run in."

In 1987, he ran right before and the day after hemorrhoid surgery. "I was in a lot of pain," he said, "but I survived."

The rules for streaks are set by each streaker. Covert sets a three-mile limit for himself, and by his standard has the world's longest active streak.

When he heard of Ron Hill crutching a single mile, Covert said, "That's getting out of hand. That's getting ridiculous.

"Does that mean if I break both my legs but push myself around in a wheelchair for three miles that my streak is still alive? I don't think so."

Don't be too quick to condemn this streaker. Other than running more often, Covert isn't much different in outlook from the rest of us.

He said, "There are no days when I get up and think, 'Gee, if I didn't have this streak I wouldn't go for a run.' That's never happened."

Like us, Covert runs because he wants to, not because he thinks he must.

Earned Rest

I never quit admiring people like Ron Hill and Mark Covert. I just quit trying to imitate them.

They would be more deserving of pity than praise if they kept their streaks alive by running only slow, safe, minimal mileage or by slogging through injury after injury. But Hill and Covert haven't cheated themselves either way.

I don't admire them just for running thousands of days in a row. I admire their being able to and wanting to go that long without missing a scheduled run.

We all seek that type of endurance, whether we're scheduled to run twice every day or three times a week. We all must compromise sometimes to keep going—to "look forward to the next run as much as ever," as Covert says he still does.

Even Hill and Covert have compromised as the years and miles have added up. Hill bowed to his age (then 53) and dropped one of his two daily workouts. Covert, in his 40s, dipped from his long-customary 100-mile weeks to 70 or 80.

Hill and Covert can rest up for the next run by running less or by spacing runs 24 hours apart instead of 12. Some of us don't rebound so quickly. We have days when *any* running is too much.

I say this as a reformed streaker. Between the late 1960s and 1987, I never willingly took a day off. My longest streak stretched for almost five years, and several others lasted two or more years.

Streaking hadn't hurt me visibly. By the Hill-Covert standards, I had endured well enough to be able and willing to run all those days in a row.

Realize that your need for rest days usually rises with age. Schedule more of them as you grow older.

The damage took a more subtle form. To keep the streak alive, I compromised.

My runs became shorter and shorter and slower and slower, and races fewer and fewer. I avoided doing whatever might keep me from running the next day. And in the process, I ran few of what made running exciting—the longer runs, the faster runs, the races.

Streaking ended in my mid-40s when I saw what was missing. I also recognized then that for me there was no longer any such thing as an "easy" run.

Any running, no matter how short and slow, left a mark that couldn't be erased overnight. Only rest could erase it.

But I couldn't take a rest any old time. It was as George Sheehan once wrote about showering: "You can't take a shower anytime you want."

Taking one without first working up a good sweat, said Sheehan, "is as gross as eating when you're not hungry or drinking when you're not thirsty." You have to earn a good drink, a good meal, and a good shower.

And I had to earn a rest with runs that were longer and faster than they'd been in the dog days of the streak. That earning took the form of a quota system.

About two hours of running, in as many days as that took, worked up my appetite for rest. Then a day of rest renewed my urge to run.

This became a new form of streaking: Doing what was needed to keep going indefinitely.

Partial Rest

Here's your dilemma for today. You're so attached to running that you want to do it every day, but to keep running well you sometimes need a day off.

Lisa Weidenbach solved this conflict by convincing herself that rest days rewarded instead of penalized her. Jack Welch wrote in *Track and Field News* that the three-time Olympic Marathon alternate "is training smarter, following a nine-day cycle. Call it a nine-day week with two extra rest days."

Weidenbach said at the time, "I haven't been injured since I started working this way three years ago. I no longer run through a twinge or a twang."

I've quit streaking but still think like a streaker. I'm torn between wanting to run daily to feel active, and needing days off to maintain health. The solution: Take the needed rest and fake the wanted run with some other activity.

On rest days, it isn't so much the running that you miss as the routine of getting up, getting dressed, getting out, and getting going. It isn't so much the activity you need to avoid as the pounding of running.

You can stay active while avoiding the pounding. You can keep the routine without the running.

> Rest completely or accept active substitutes. Walk, swim, or bike on "rest days" if you wish—just stay away from running's pounding.

My routine never bores me. Nothing short of hospitalization need ever interrupt it.

On "rest" days, I do everything the normal way: get up and out early, dress as if running, wear running shoes, use a runner's watch, follow the same courses, stay out for the same length of time.

Except that I don't run but simply walk. You might choose to bike, swim, or "run" in a pool.

Take your pick of the many suitable alternatives, but don't even try to mimic the effort of running. This day is supposed to be easier than yesterday was.

Run daily if you want to and are able to do it. But don't strain to streak when a substitute activity today can keep you moving while easing you into a better run tomorrow.

Masters Rest

Bill Meyer had tried training the other way. "I had gone as high as 100 miles per week," wrote the runner from Pennsylvania, "yet I was unable to break 1:30 for the half-marathon or 3:30 for the marathon."

Then he read the Bill Rodgers and Priscilla Welch book, *Masters Running and Racing*. Meyer put their advice to work for himself.

He mainly heeded their line about why masters need to adjust their approach: "An older runner gets hurt quicker and heals slower than a younger one." That hurting extends to the subtle, sub-injury damage done by races and hard workouts.

Performances don't necessarily fall off in the masters years. Welch is proof of that. She ran the fastest 10K of her life at 40 and her best marathon at 42.

When you stop improving is less a function of how old you are than when you started racing. Runners of any age have 5 to 10 years of improvement in them.

Times don't inevitably slow down with age. But recovery rates almost invariably do.

You can train hard as a master, and you might even run farther and faster than ever before. You just can't do this too often.

A 20-year-old can run to the limit, take two or three deep breaths, and do the same thing all over again. Youth is forgiving that way.

A 40-year-old might run exactly the same distance and pace as the kid, but then might need to take two or three easy days before repeating that effort.

Priscilla Welch denied in the book (written in 1990) that the years had slowed her. But she admitted, "My recovery isn't quite what it used

© Ken Lee

Priscilla Welch, top masters runner, has been able to lengthen her career by planning rest cycles into her training.

to be. My husband-coach Dave and I have adjusted my weekly program to allow for this.

"I used to schedule a heavy training day on Tuesday, a long run on Wednesday, and another quality workout on Thursday. Three days of heavy training in a row is a bit much to ask of my body."

Plan to rest more as your program intensifies. Add a day off each week during marathon training, for instance.

Bill Rodgers wrote, "You can't recover as well at 40 or 41 as you did 10 years before. You're not as resilient. You can't bounce back as quickly.

"When I was training my best in the late 1970s, I averaged 130 miles a week for three years. I can't do that anymore without risking injury."

This advice led Bill Meyer to mend his own high-mileage ways. He immediately began to write a whole new set of personal records.

In his late 40s, he set half-marathon and marathon PRs of 1:25 and 3:17 in quick succession. His wife Maureen also PRed in those same events.

"After those races," said Bill, "we were besieged with questions of, 'How did you do it?' We both defeated longtime race foes, and they wanted to know how they could improve as we had.

"My answer: reduced total mileage, three good workouts (intervals on Tuesday, tempo run on Friday, long run on Sunday), and rest or easy runs the other four days."

Masters must accept the slower recovery timetable, Bill Rodgers wrote in their book. "You can't tell yourself you aren't aging. God made us this way."

But nature provides tradeoffs, Priscilla Welch added. "Our recovery from hard efforts may not be quite as fast as it was before. But we compensate on the emotional side. Our strength is our ability to concentrate and endure."

Pre-Race Rest

On its surface, the following appears to be a story about swimming. But it is equally a story about running because of who the swimmer is, how he took lessons learned as a runner into the pool, and what advice he now hands back to our sport.

Dr. David Costill first made his name as an exercise physiologist by studying runners at the now-famous Human Performance Laboratory at Ball State University. However, his own running ended in the early 1980s when his knees rebelled. He then returned to his original sport, swimming.

"I had quit swimming after competing at Ohio University," said Costill, "because that was what swimmers did then—retire early. I wanted to stay active in some way after graduation, decided to start running, and kept doing it for almost 20 years."

Then came injuries to both knees, and Costill began swimming only for fitness. But soon he was racing again—not only competing but doing better than he had in college, and not only better against men his age but better against the clock.

For instance: "My best 200-yard freestyle at age 21 was 2:07. My average time at age 51 was about 1:59."

One reason for the improvement was mechanical. "Stroke technique had changed over the years," said Costill, "and I picked up the new patterns."

But mainly he had improved his training. "I've been able to put to use some of the practical lessons from running and the laboratory. The main one is to train according to how I feel each day, judging when to push or back off.

"You have to be realistic about how much the body can adapt to and how much stimulus you need to produce the most adaptation. That differs, of course, from one person to another. But the majority of elite-level swimmers could probably get by on about one-fourth of the yardage they are doing."

Costill knew when to work and when to rest. "A final factor in my second-life improvement as a swimmer," he said, "was that I'd learned a lot over the years about how to rest up for competition.

"In swimming, you can taper for up to three weeks by just warming up every day. If I tried to compete without tapering this way, then my times were almost identical to what I swam in college."

In running terms, he added, a marathoner might schedule the last long run three weeks before the race. Costill wouldn't expect us to train down that long before every race, of course, but did advise running very easily or resting at least three days before every event.

Post-Race Rest

My marathon at the Drake Relays finished less than a mile from where it had started a few hours earlier. The race had ended, and we runners had stood around and stiffened up for awhile.

When the party ended, we had to limp back to where we'd parked our cars. The 27th mile would be the longest of our day.

It would also begin the phase of marathon training that most programs downplay or ignore altogether. The part that began at the finish line would determine when or if we would run this distance again.

A marathon is exciting to think about, challenging to run, and satisfying to recall. But it's also an injury that marathoners inflict upon themselves.

Take extra rest before and after a race—one day on either side, and more if the event is extra-demanding.

Full recovery takes several weeks. First aid must begin immediately.

It starts with a quick change of clothes. Get out of the cool and wet, and into the warm and dry, or you'll risk chilling as the apparent temperature—how it *feels* to you—plunges by 20 or 30 degrees within minutes.

You might not have eaten or drunk anything caloric since the night before. So start force-feeding the carbos as soon as possible.

Carbohydrate *reloading* is more vital than the loading ever was. You were only topping off the energy tank before, but now the gauge registers "empty."

Don't miss the post-race partying. But don't avoid walking the 27th mile, either. It's important if only to assure yourself that you can still move in some fashion at least under your own power.

Resist the temptation to soak in a bathtub. The muscles are overheated already, and the hot water will increase the inflammation and slow recovery.

Cold water would do you more good, but I'm not sadistic enough to suggest bathing that way. Just take a quick, warm shower.

This day and the next, wear your accomplishment proudly. Leave your time on your watch, and take pride in knowing that you put every hour, minute, and second there. Show off your soreness as a badge of courage.

You'll soon discover how little the people around you care about what you did. The family will start to wonder, "When will things get back to normal around here?"

To be polite, friends will ask, "How long was this marathon you ran?" After you explain that marathons only come in one size, you'll hear,

"Did you win?" You did, of course, but not in a way most people understand winning.

Two days after the race, you'll hit bottom. Soreness will peak then.

You were intoxicated with self-satisfaction before. Now comes the hangover, otherwise known as "post-marathon blues."

This affliction serves a purpose. It keeps you from coming back too soon and doing too much.

You want to eat more than usual, drink more, sleep more. Listen to your body and indulge yourself.

Don't try to run off the soreness. Don't think that by running you'll "flush out the lactic acid," because this isn't your problem. It's overpounded and overtired muscles.

Dr. David Costill, the master tester of athletes, once measured the recovery rates of runners who ran versus those who rested after a marathon. The resters won easily.

Three or four days after the marathon, the stiffness will have eased. You'll be ready to run again, if not entirely willing. The first careful mile leading to your next race starts here.

6

Better

Schedules

Ask me, "How was your run today?" or, "What kind of shoes do you prefer?" or, "Have you lost weight?" I'll answer you in a second and be your friend for life.

This was another of those simple icebreaker questions between runner strangers who are about to become friends. She asked, "How many miles per week do you run?"

"Uh . . . hmm . . . well," I stammered. I didn't have a clue.

You see, I haven't counted weekly miles since the 1960s. And it has been years since I've scheduled my running by weeks.

When I've suggested in stories and talks that runners stop counting their miles and run instead by time periods, my audiences have reacted as if I were trying to pull the ground out from under them. When I now tell them to go off their weekly schedules, they respond as if I'd recommended canceling Christmas.

Please understand that I have no real quarrel with miles. It's just simpler to run by the watch, which tells exactly how long you're out while freeing you from plotting and measuring courses.

Run by miles or by time. Either way is fine. Just take care to avoid the deadly combination of a known distance and an accurate time that can lure you into racing all of your training.

My real argument isn't with miles but with weeks. A weekly count of mileage (or time, if you prefer) is the most misleading number that runners quote.

Weeks are both too short and too long. They're too brief to give an accurate accounting, because one extra-long or extra-short day in seven can badly skew the total without seriously affecting your fitness. A *monthly* record would give a truer picture of what you've accomplished.

A week is also too long for most of us to go without a break. Which brings us to the heart of the problem with weekly counts: They penalize you for resting or even easing off.

Two things are likely to happen when you count by the week. The routine can flatten, and the rest days can disappear.

Say you're aiming to run 50-mile weeks. The simplest way to do this is to put in about seven miles on each of the seven days.

Those seven miles might be too long on the days that should be easier and too short on the days that should be harder. You might never increase the pace for fear of sacrificing mileage.

The main problem, however, is that you might not take what you need the most—a day off. It would leave a big fat zero in your logbook that you'd have to correct by adding miles to other days.

Two tricks can correct these shortcomings while still satisfying our compulsion to count:

1. *Replace weekly totals with daily averages.* I prefer to average by the month instead of by the week, but choose whichever period seems right for you. Add up your running during that period, then divide that total only by the number of days when you ran. The averaging system removes the penalty for resting, but still tempts you to flatten the routine. A better system, and my choice for the past several years, is . . .

2. *Toss out the seven-day week and replace it with a quota system.* Set as a quota an amount equal to the longest run you'd take in a typical month. Say it's two hours. Run as many days as needed to total those two hours, then take the day off that you've earned before starting a new cycle.

Now if someone would just ask, "How many hours per cycle do you run?" I'd have an answer.

Three-Day Schedule

"What's new this year?" I asked Jeff Galloway as we sat down together at his Squaw Valley running camp. This wasn't an idle conversation-opener. Each year, Galloway comes up with an idea worth considering.

© Ken Lee

Jeff Galloway now runs on a three-day schedule: a long, slow run one day, a short, fast run the second day, and an easy or rest day the third.

One year, he introduced me to his marathon-training program, which (with a few alterations) I now use and recommend. A few years later, he eased that program's longest runs by adding walking breaks.

Jeff's minuscule body fat makes him about as buoyant and as cold-resistant as a rock, yet he was one of the first writers to promote water-running. Bicycling on the streets terrifies him, but one summer when I asked, he told of training for a triathlon.

Shortly after turning 40, Jeff found that he wasn't recovering well from one day to the next. So in another of his innovations he went to every-other-day runs.

He didn't get me to go along all the way with that idea. I liked running too well to do it only half the days. But his arguments did convince me to break a five-year rest-less streak and take *some* days off.

Galloway answered my latest what's-new question by saying, "I'm not running every other day anymore." This didn't mean he now ran even less often but that he'd found a way to run more days between rests.

"Like you," he explained, "I always felt something was missing if I only ran three or four days a week. I always wanted to run more often but couldn't find the right combination that would let me do that productively."

Jeff had never stopped running hard. His run days featured both quantity and quality. He came to see that his long runs had been too fast and his fast runs too long to allow quick recovery.

Simplify your schedule. Boil it down to the few basic sessions that you need most and like best.

Good ideas can be slow to sprout, even in a fertile mind like Jeff Galloway's. He had planted this seed more than 10 years earlier, when he still trained twice most days and still could run near his best marathon time of 2:15.

Galloway wrote then in a triathlon magazine about alternating the stresses. He suggested training for the swim one day, the bike the next, and then the run before beginning the same rotation again.

He also told at that time how to extend this three-day cycle to running training: a long and slow run one day, a short and fast one the next, an easy one or rest the next. He said the days are so different that someone could handle them more easily in this sequence than by running the same way day after day.

The long-slow and short-fast runs use different muscles, different rhythms. This way you don't run exactly the same way more than once every third day.

Galloway liked this idea well enough in theory to write about it in the early 1980s. But he waited until the '90s to practice it.

He moderated the pace of the long runs. "I might run eight or nine minutes a mile," he confessed with an embarrassed grin. This is a guy who once made the Olympic 10,000-meter team.

He made up for that slow pace the next day, when, he said, "I run something very different. I go fast, using a different stride and fresh muscles that weren't overworked on the long run. But I keep the distance short so I can maintain a good speed and yet not overtax myself."

On the third day, he runs nothing. Jeff had learned in an earlier year that rest days are a key element in the training equation. Now he was happy to report that their value in his puzzle has dropped from one-half to one-third.

Rotating Schedule

Hal Higdon, America's senior running writer, added fuel to the discussion of running two days out of three. Instead of alternating 24- and 48-hour rests between workouts, as Jeff Galloway had suggested, Higdon recommended running every 36 hours.

This pattern involves training in the morning one day and the afternoon the next. His approach still shook out, as Galloway's did, to taking every third day off.

Let's now ease the fear that you'll run less in total and less well if you rest this much. Galloway answered that concern long ago when he first switched to less-frequent running. He didn't sacrifice any mileage, and he actually gained speed.

He compensated for training half as often by doubling the distance of each run. His racing times immediately improved because he ran longer per run and because he entered his races more rested.

Everyday running has a flattening effect on mileage. The surest way to log the miles is to run about the same number each day, but this isn't the *best* way.

Consistent daily mileage pressures you to run too much on days that should be easier—which leaves you too tired to run enough on days that should be harder. You string together too many short, same-paced, unproductive, unsatisfying runs. The whole program goes flat without variety, and without days off.

Adopt a standard rotation of long run, fast run, rest. Have a different experience each day of the cycle.

In recent years, I found that running the same way for even four or five *days* in a row flattened my running. Most of these runs were so short and slow that they barely woke me up in the morning. The only real excitement came in the faster run that ended each running cycle.

Jeff Galloway's three-day plan corrected this problem. He made a convincing case for the way it makes each of those days very different from the others.

My cycle now starts with a longer run than before. I follow a day later with a shorter, faster run.

On Jeff's plan, I run no less than before but just divide up the running differently. I'm much happier with the results, which aren't measured in race times but in terms of better health and a brighter outlook.

The three-day cycle ends with a rest day. Then this rotation starts again.

"Rotation" is a key word here. I liken the effects of alternating runs to the benefits of rotating shoes.

I once would wear a pair every day from the time I took them out of the box to their retirement. Then I'd buy a new pair just like them and wear them from infancy to death. This grooved me to run only in those shoes, and the slightest change—even from an old to a new pair—put me at risk.

Every shoe is flawed. Or maybe I should say that every *runner* is flawed, and the shoe locates and nibbles at the problem. Multiply a little irregularity times hundreds of steps per mile, then times dozens of runs per month, and the little problem can grow into a major one.

Rotating two or three different pairs of shoes eases this risk by spreading the stresses around. The feet and legs never get worked exactly the same way day after day.

Rotating different types of running has a similar effect. Each has its own peculiar stresses, and you're better off dealing with them intermittently instead of constantly. On Galloway's (and Hal Higdon's) plan, you only take a long run or a fast run every third day.

Once every three days, you also rest. This may be the hardest part of the cycle for you to swallow.

If you can't face a day without a workout, do something other than running. Swim or run in water, hike or bike, or do household chores. But don't waste energy doing a short, slow run when a longer or faster one is just a day away.

> Rarely run the same way two days in a row. And rarely take more than two straight days of rest.

Marathon Schedule

Runners training for a marathon form my favorite audiences. No group listens more intently, or more critically, to my talks than these runners who are all headed for the same destination but are still mapping their routes to it.

Each year, I speak at clinics preparing marathoners for the Portland, Los Angeles, and Long Beach races that will come months later. Each year, I learn as much from these runners as they do from me.

I've already learned how stubbornly they cling to the most misleading number in their logbooks. This count adds little to training and can take away a lot.

At Long Beach one winter, I spoke to runners pointing for that city's marathon. The talk included my usual reformed-streaker's appeal to take one day off a week.

"When you're taking longer long runs for a marathon," I said, "you probably need an *extra* rest day each week to compensate."

During question time, a woman from the audience said, "I see your point about days off. But I'm afraid to take any because they hurt my weekly mileage."

My answer: "I don't just want to hurt it. I'd like to help *kill* it."

It's the mile-counting that hurts. To stop the hurting, we have to quit keeping score this way.

The damage takes many forms, from subtle to serious. At the least, your program flattens to same-distance-every-day as the simplest way to meet the weekly quota. Or, at worst, you refuse to take the "penalty" of what you may need most: a day off.

Jeff Galloway, who routinely filled 140-mile weeks while training for the 1972 Olympics, now leads the move away from mile-counting. When Galloway began giving advice to new marathoners a decade ago, he didn't ask them to go to his lengths but did urge them to keep a count.

Jeff at that time still followed the "collapse-point theory." It predicts that the Wall will arrive at triple a runner's average daily training distance.

Under this theory, a marathoner needs to average nearly nine miles a day—or 60-plus a week. Galloway's original program, along with mine and many others from that era, thus listed 60 miles a week as the minimum.

Runners by the thousands trained this way. Most finished their marathons.

But a disturbing number broke down from pain and fatigue, some of them in the race itself but more in the training period. Galloway reviewed the bad experiences reported to him and concluded that "the program asked people to run too much without running enough."

Keep score by average length of runs instead of weekly total. Take no penalties for days without running.

Mile-counting pressures you to run too much on days when you need less. Then it leaves you too tired or sore to run enough on days when you need more running.

Jeff Galloway hasn't become antidistance, and neither have I. We both emphasize it more than ever.

Only now, the emphasis is better placed: on an occasional high-mileage *day*, not on more miles per week. Galloway's revised program (now the most-followed in the sport) contains longer long runs than before, but also fewer of them, plus shorter short runs and more days of nothing.

Jeff now tells marathoners to push each of their long training runs closer to marathon length. Then spend two weeks rebuilding for the next big effort by cutting mileage, not adding it up.

7

Better

Results

Having just preached against counting miles (in chapter 6), I must confess to being an unrepentant counter. I don't count miles; don't count by the week but by the month; don't count a monthly total but a daily average—but I do keep counting.

I've done this counting every month for most of 35 years of diary keeping. My most important book is the personal journal that no one else ever sees.

The most important line in that diary is the first one each day. Words fill the page, but the vital record appears as a single number at the top.

That number reports the day's run by time. Any one day leaves behind only a random footprint in the diary, but in time these prints link up.

A month's worth of days, a year's worth of months, a decade's worth of years mark a clear path. The diary-trail serves both as a record of past travels and a roadmap for those to come.

Written Results

Ken Newhams works with computers, but he's more than a number cruncher. He writes prose along with computer programs, and the written work appears in several running publications.

"Shame on you as a writer for suggesting that a running diary may contain no words," Newhams wrote in response to the preceding piece, which seemed to say that numbers might be all you need to record. "The best words I write come during and after my runs."

I too think up lines while running and write them down afterward. I've done this daily since the 1950s.

The diary, begun as a place to record distances and times, soon did much more. It taught me to write.

Most of this writing, now totaling thousands of pages, will never see print. But it all has served a purpose that numbers alone can't satisfy.

Numbers summarize facts, but say nothing about feelings, which only words can express. Numbers are the brain of a running diary, and words are its heart.

Many runners share with Ken Newhams and me the compulsion to write notes to ourselves on diary pages. The diary's ultimate value is not as a storehouse for facts but as a collection of memories. You can open it to any old page and bring a day back to life.

You don't need professional writing talent to profit from a diary. Just as running is too valuable to leave to the fast runners, writing is too good to belong strictly to the slick writers.

You may not have their skill at wordplay. But just as paid runners can't run your races for you, neither can published writers write your stories. If you want to be the subject of a biography, you must be your own biographer.

Beginning to write is as simple as starting to run. Anyone who walks can run, and anyone who talks can write.

But first you have to clear two mental blocks: "I" phobia and perfection syndrome.

Lose the fear of writing the first-person pronoun a half-dozen times per paragraph. The diary is your book, you're its star, and modesty has no place here.

Exercise your ego in the diary. When you're free to talk about yourself, you should never be at a loss for words.

Writers only block up when they try to write too perfectly—when they put style before content, or when they feel the eyes of a critic looking over their shoulder. You work best by putting pen to paper and letting the stream of consciousness flow for an audience of one.

Pour your feelings onto the page. Make note of special people met and experiences had, of your dreams and plans, your hopes and fears, joys and frustrations. Let your observations and opinions fly, because you can't shock or bore anyone in this private book.

Write a diary. Fill it with running results, but also record ideas and impressions in your own words.

Here rest the fresh ideas going onto paper for the first time, and they're beautiful. These imperfect lines mark the exact point where running ends and remembering begins.

This page becomes the most lasting part of the run. It gives substance to events that, if left unrecorded, would be as invisible as footprints left behind on the pavement.

Metric Results

A column of mine once asked why we run races at metric distances if we persist in taking splits and quoting paces by the mile. Let's go one way or the other, I suggested—all the way back to miles or ahead to meters.

I know of just one race that mended its ways as a result of that piece. A former five-miler became an 8K, and splits came only at kilometer points.

Runners hated the second change, calling the metric splits "meaningless." Mileposts returned by popular demand the next year—for a race that remains an 8K.

My case for meters has little to do with its making more sense mathematically than the old British measurements or with joining the rest of the world (including the Brits, who've abandoned the system they invented). I don't care if we know the difference between Celsius and cellulite, liters and litters, or grams and grahams.

My arguments for metric distances deal entirely with their simple, practical, measurable benefits to runners. Since this is a decimal-based system, I list 10 of its beauties.

1. *Math becomes simpler.* During a 10K race, you simply double the 5K split to project your final time instead of fumbling for a 6.2-mile time from a 3-mile split. After this 10K race, you can compute pace per kilometer in your head instead of needing a calculator to divide your time by 6.2 miles.

2. *Distances sound longer.* An 8K race somehow seems more substantial than a 5-miler and a 50K training week sounds more impressive than one of 30 miles, though the distances are almost identical.

3. *Paces sound faster.* Racing at 4:00 per kilometer has a nicer ring to it than the comparable 6:30 per mile, and so does training with five-minute kilometers rather than eight-minute miles.

4. *Kilometers add up faster.* You reach round-number landmarks—such as a run of 10, a month of 100, or a year of 1,000—almost 40 percent sooner with kilometers than with miles.

5. *Splits come up more often.* A race distance feels as if it passes more quickly when the metric checkpoints appear nearly twice as often as mileposts do.

6. *Training distances become realistic.* Few of us could tolerate the 100-mile weeks that once were the rage, and 50-mile weeks were a push. But 100 kilometers are within reach, and 50 kilometers are reasonable.

7. *Fast runs become faster.* I've long promoted a 1-1 plan—one-mile runs at one minute faster than normal training pace. A metric 1-1 cuts the distance of these intervals and ups their speed.

8. *Easy runs become easier.* The effort of running a minute per kilometer slower than race pace is noticeably less than backing off by only a minute per mile.

9. *Long runs become longer.* If taking walking breaks can extend distances, then walks averaging one minute per kilometer will give more of a stretch than breaks of one minute per mile.

10. *Race spacing becomes wider.* The well-used formula is to allow one day of recovery for each mile of the race, which may not be enough if you are older or you race really hard. One day per kilometer will give you two extra weeks to get over a marathon.

> Use metric measurements, if only because they make distances sound longer and paces sound faster.

Projected Results

"Set realistic goals," the running advisers tell us. The quickest way to discourage yourself, they say, is to choose a target you can never hit.

So what is "realistic"? If you raced the same distance every week, you would know.

But today's runners flit from distance to distance. Between 5K and the half-marathon, we can choose among nine different standard events.

What do recent times at one distance tell you about your potential results at other distances? For almost as long as I've been running, I have looked for answers to that question. I've drawn graphs and constructed tables that bogged down in complex calculations.

I was no better at explaining these conversions than calculating them. After I had tried and failed at a running clinic many years ago, a man from the audience said, "It really isn't as complicated as you make it. All you need to do is add five percent to the pace each time you double your distance, or subtract five percent at half the distance."

> Project your racing potential from one distance to another with simple math (using the formulas in this chapter).

The man's formula appeared to work, but the calculations were still cumbersome. They stayed that way until Mike Tymn simplified the five-percent rule.

"Concerning your race predictions," said Tymn, a columnist for *National Masters News*, "you might consider approaching them this way." He then converted five percent to a multiplier or divisor of 2.1.

"Although a marathon is twice as long as a half-marathon," Tymn wrote, "the average difference between the times of well-conditioned runners is 2.1."

For example, a person capable of a 1:30 half should be able to run a 3:09 marathon (90 minutes times 2.1 equals 189 minutes). A 3:00 marathoner should be capable of running a 1:26 half (180 minutes divided by 2.1 equals 86 minutes).

From this formula, we can pick fractions or multiples of 2.1 to fit any combination of distances. I've done some of that figuring for you, for both track and road races. Multiply or divide by the factor listed for your set of distances:

Track Races

(*Multiply* the shorter-distance time by the factor indicated to project longer-distance time. *Divide* the longer-distance time by the factor indicated to project shorter-distance time.)

Distances to compare	Multiply/divide by*
1,500m and mile	1.08
1,500m and 3,000m	2.10
Mile and 3,000m	1.98
Mile and 2 miles	2.10
3,000m and 5,000m	1.56
5,000m and 10,000m	2.10

These calculations don't just satisfy your curiosity about the future. More important, they serve as pacing guidelines for upcoming races.

You can't know in advance exactly how any race will end. But knowing what you can expect to run gives you a better idea how to *start*.

Base your race plans on the projected time. If, for instance, you predict a 10K time of 40 minutes, or about 6:30 per mile, start at a 6:30-mile pace.

Formulas such as this can help you set realistic goals, and then plan training and pacing accordingly. They can provide road maps for unfamiliar racing territory.

Road Races

(*Multiply* the shorter-distance time by the factor indicated to project longer-distance time. *Divide* the longer-distance time by the factor indicated to project shorter-distance time.)

Distances to compare	Multiply/divide by*
5K and 5 miles or 8K	1.66
5K and 10K	2.10
5 miles and 10K	1.28
5 miles and 15K	1.97
5 miles and 10 miles	2.10
10K and 15K	1.55
10K and 10 miles	1.68
10K and 20K	2.10
15K and 10 miles	1.08
15K and 20K	1.37
15K and half-marathon	1.45
15K and 25K	1.74
10 miles and 20K	1.27
10 miles and half-marathon	1.34
10 miles and 25K	1.61
20K and half-marathon	1.06
20K and 25K	1.28
Half-marathon and 25K	1.20
Half- and full-marathon	2.10
25K and marathon	1.76

However, don't let the numbers place artificial limits on performance or remove the element of surprise from your final results. Exploring the unknown and unknowable is a major reason to race.

Age-Graded Results

Given my vintage, I now spend much of my time talking with middle-aged and older runners. Most of them complain about not being the runners they used to be.

Several of us shared dinner after the George Sheehan Classic 10K. We either dodged the question of "How did you do?" or apologized to one another for our slowness.

One of my tablemates had run in an Olympic Marathon Trial. Even her times hadn't escaped the erosion of the years.

Nobody escapes for good. Not Eamonn Coghlan, whose sub-four-minute mile as a master was still nine seconds away from his PR. Not

Shirley Matson achieves better results as a masters runner.

even 42-year-old Yekaterina Podkopayeva, whose falloff at 1,500 meters was a minuscule three seconds in 10 years.

We all eventually slow down. But there is a better way to live with that decline than denying or apologizing for it. We can learn to read times differently.

One of the most comforting books ever written on running contains mostly numbers. It is the *Age-Graded Tables*, first issued in the 1980s and regularly updated.

This is the best way yet to judge the historical merit of race times. The World Association of Veteran Athletes (WAVA) designed these tables mainly to compare the various age-groups at track meets and road races, but the book's greatest value is personal. It answers the question, "Am I slowing down too fast?"

WAVA's computer generated the tables by comparing open-class world records (nearly all of them set by runners in their early 20s to mid-30s) with single-age marks. These figures make allowances for marks like Podkopayeva's and Coghlan's that stand far above the normal curve, and certain older-age records that fall well below it.

These calculations yield a percentage figure for each event, age, and sex. Multiplying your time by this four-digit factor tells what you theoretically would have run in your prime years, which WAVA lists as 20 to 34 for most long-distance races.

An example of how this scoring works: A 50-year-old woman runs a 10K in 48:06. Her magic number is 87.92 percent. She multiplies her time by that age factor and learns that she might have run 42:18 as a younger runner, according to the *Age-Graded Tables*.

That book does the math for you. Some calculations can give startling, if not ridiculous, results. Podkopayeva is off the charts, as her converted 3:41 1,500 is 9 seconds under the world record and 15 better than her PR.

Coghlan also looks better than ever in his 40s. His mile time equates to 3:42, or two seconds below the world mark and a PR by seven.

Remember, though, that the scoring factors are based on normal slowdown rates. These two runners aren't normal.

The closer you are to the norms, the better the age-graded tables work. I believe in them for myself, even though they let age forgive less than half of my slowdown.

Since my PRs ended in the 1960s, the years alone have penalized me about a minute for every mile. The rest of the loss is my own fault.

Age-Graded Scoring (Women)

Here is a sample of the tables that fill 60 pages of the booklet compiled by the World Association of Veteran Athletes (WAVA) and published by *National Masters News*. Multiply your time for one of the racing distances listed by the grading factor that most closely matches your current age. The result is your age-graded time.

Age	Women's grading factors			
	5K	10K	H-M	Marathon
10	.8553	.8434	.8251	.8134
15	.9647	.9591	.9499	.9432
20	1.000	1.000	1.000	1.000
25	1.000	1.000	1.000	1.000
30	1.000	1.000	1.000	1.000
35	.9913	.9974	1.000	1.000
40	.9525	.9585	.9657	.9745
45	.9133	.9192	.9263	.9351
50	.8734	.8792	.8862	.8950
55	.8324	.8381	.8450	.8538
60	.7898	.7954	.8022	.8110
65	.7450	.7505	.7572	.7660
70	.6973	.7027	.7093	.7181
75	.6459	.6512	.6577	.6665
80	.5897	.5949	.6013	.6101

From *Age-Graded Tables*. Compiled by the World Association of Veteran Athletes. Available from *National Masters News*, Box 2372, Van Nuys, CA 91404. Adapted with permission.

Age-Graded Scoring (Men)

Here is a sample of the tables that fill 60 pages of the booklet compiled by the World Association of Veteran Athletes (WAVA) and published by *National Masters News*. Multiply your time for one of the racing distances listed by the grading factor that most closely matches your current age. The result is your age-graded time.

	Men's grading factors			
Age	**5K**	**10K**	**H-M**	**Marathon**
10	.8496	.8588	.8524	.8346
15	.9543	.9570	.9531	.9452
20	1.000	1.000	1.000	1.000
25	1.000	1.000	1.000	1.000
30	1.000	1.000	1.000	1.000
35	.9963	1.000	1.000	1.000
40	.9624	.9679	.9751	.9835
45	.9281	.9333	.9404	.9486
50	.8931	.8980	.9050	.9130
55	.8570	.8616	.8685	.8763
60	.8193	.8236	.8304	.8380
65	.7794	.7834	.7901	.7975
70	.7366	.7403	.7469	.7541
75	.6901	.6935	.7000	.7070
80	.6388	.6419	.6483	.6551

From *Age-Graded Tables*. Compiled by the World Association of Veteran Athletes. Available from *National Masters News*, Box 2372, Van Nuys, CA 91404. Adapted with permission.

Record Results

PRs—personal records—are one of this sport's great inventions. They mean you don't have to beat everyone—or anyone—to win a race. You can win by improving your time. The trouble with times, though, is that they sometimes lie.

Back when stopwatches still had hands and course measurement was done by car odometer, I set two personal records too good to be true. I improved my high school half-mile time by four seconds and my best six-mile (the 10K of yesteryear) by two minutes. I accepted the times without question as PRs.

Only after they taunted me for several years, refusing to be broken, did I accept the truth. The stopwatch that I'd carried in the half-mile had surely stopped too soon. The six-mile must have fallen well short of full distance.

Keep your PRs pure. Weed out those set with unfair advantages such as tailwinds or downhill slopes.

Watches work better now, and courses are accurate to the centimeter. But the people holding the watches still err, and certain types of courses still inflate PRs.

I've had reason lately to see more high school races than at any time since my own schooldays. What strikes me most is how little the kids' thinking has changed there in a generation. They still view their PRs the way I did a generation ago, wanting to believe whatever the watch tells them.

I saw my son Eric celebrate a big PR. My watch gave him a much slower time than the "official" clocking by a volunteer who'd never held a watch before, but the young runner wanted desperately to believe the rookie timer.

I suggested that Eric take the slower time, hard as that was to accept in his moment of elation. If he didn't, the false time would come back to haunt him in later races. He wouldn't run that fast again and might think he had failed—even while breaking his true PR.

Inflated times don't just lay traps for kids. All runners want very much to believe the best news a watch can offer.

At the 1994 Boston Marathon, the times benefited doubly from slope and wind. The course descended at more than three times the limit for national road records. Boston officials downplayed the wind readings, but TV coverage of the race showed the long hair of runners blowing forward.

Never before had so many men and women run so fast. Maybe too fast.

How these times appear on record lists doesn't concern me so much as how these times might haunt and taunt the runners later. Everyone who ran fast in Boston now wanted to think this new level was his or her true one.

What happened the next time the countless Boston PR-setters ran under neutral conditions? They probably ran their normal times and wondered, "What went wrong?"

The only way to beat inflated time might be to seek out ever-more-helpful routes. Runners who choose to believe that times from such aided courses are true PRs can prepare to live in their shadow. These might well be the last records they ever set.

One way to keep PRs breakable is to expand the lists. Keep one set for unaided conditions and another for assisted races, as the national record screeners do. Or start a new list at key turning points in life, such as entry into a fresh 10-year age group.

Records are made to be broken. They serve no purpose by becoming unbreakable.

II

Running and Racing

8

Better

Paces

One of the greatest advances in running technology is so small, cheap, and common that we take it for granted. It has become as essential a piece of equipment as shoes.

It's the digital wrist-stopwatch, fashioned of electronic gadgetry and encased in plastic. Before its invention, we never really knew the time.

We carried hand-held stopwatches that had an infuriating habit of stopping before the runs did. Or we wore wristwatches with hands and guessed at a time as they moved.

Timing this rough didn't mean much. So we trained by the mile, which meant using only measured courses. And we raced for place, which meant that few runners placed high enough to feel like winners.

The digitals freed us from these standards. They let us measure training by time periods, which passed at the same rate on any course. And this new means of checking times gave everyone a way to win at races: instant and accurate evidence of personal records.

These watches certainly changed the way we start and finish races. Runners used to begin with hands on knees and end by flinging both arms up in a victory salute. Now the classic pose at either end is a finger on the start/stop button.

Digitals have evolved in a way unique to electronic devices: increasingly cheaper, smaller, and simpler. The first ones, made of heavy metal and needing a course in computer science to operate, sold for about $300.

My latest Casio cost $14, and I've bought others on sale for half that much. Any technophobe can make it work.

No running product gives greater value per dollar than this watch. At your fingertip, it puts the power to make your own time, to make time stand still, and to make time disappear.

You put every minute, second, and fraction on the watch through your own effort. The numbers on the watch are visual proof of work that otherwise would have disappeared behind you like footprints on the beach.

You freeze time on the watch. Training times and racing results stay just where they were when you finished, there on the face to glance at and feel proud of long after the run is done.

© Photo Run/Victor Sailer

Runners await the gun to start the 1992 Olympic marathon trials.

You wipe time away with the watch. It provides graphic evidence that your efforts, no matter how good, are fleeting and must be replaced. The next run always starts again at "0:00.00."

Pretending to make time stop and go at will is, of course, as artificial as the watch is synthetic. But if running is just a game, what's wrong with using this toy to play it?

Slower Paces

My partner in life is sometimes amused, sometimes irritated at my all-or-nothing mentality. Barbara says, "You see everything in blacks and whites, as either/or."

This affliction is a defining trait of runners. We tend to be extremists by nature.

We either run all speed or all distance, always or never on roads. We train every day without fail or take every other day off, race weekly or not at all. We stretch religiously or avoid it completely, watch our diets or ignore them.

I've swung to all these extremes and more. But now I've found some balance between two of them: between timing every mile and timing none.

The watch once was my enemy. I always ran against time, and it usually moved too fast for me.

> Check times for known distances only sparingly. Avoid turning every training run into a course-record attempt.

We made peace in 1966. I began running *with* time instead of against it, running by time periods instead of miles, running without knowing the pace per mile.

Mixing a known distance with an accurate time poses risks to an extremist runner's physical and mental health. It urges you to force the pace and then depresses you when the time is slower than hoped.

Running either a measured distance untimed or a time for unchecked mileage avoids this problem. Not knowing how fast or how far you're going removes the pressures or temptations to race your training.

Choosing time over distance has practical advantages. Time lets you run anywhere without having to plot a course. An hour takes an hour wherever the run takes you, so running by time periods encourages exploring.

An hour's run also takes an hour to complete no matter what your pace is, but it *seems* longer if the effort is forced. Time-period running encourages settling into your most comfortable pace.

But mine has grown a little too relaxed over the years. Pace is like weight. If you don't watch it, it creeps up on you.

While not tracking my everyday pace, I let it slip little by little for a long time until the total now is enormous. I'd imagined it to be about a minute per mile slower than in the 1960s, but recent checks have put the difference at two minutes or more.

This slippage was mildly shocking. It means that my longest training runs of 25 years ago went faster than my shortest races do today.

Age is only partly to blame for this loss. Also figuring into it is neglect.

Some of the time is lost forever, and I don't mourn it. But some can be reclaimed by timing some miles again.

Going off the pace-per-mile standard once served to put the brakes on training that went too fast. I now need these times back as a nudge to go a little faster.

Spot-check your pace occasionally during longer runs. Time yourself only for a measured mile or so.

The idea here isn't to trade one extreme for the other. It isn't to go from timing no miles to timing them all. It's this:

- Run basically by minutes because they're more practical than miles. But make spot-checks of pace on a track or a measured stretch of road.

- Time a distance as short as a quarter-mile or as long as a mile, and don't speed up or the reading will be false. Check the pace in mid-run, not at the start or end where pacing is the least normal.

- Learn what that norm is without making an either/or choice. Combine the best of both time and distance.

Faster Paces

Something went wrong with me mechanically. My timing was off and needed adjusting.

The faster runs that I took every few days no longer had their intended effects. They were supposed to lift my spirits and liven my legs, but I now felt dread before these runs and dead afterward.

The problem was time. I no longer controlled it. It ran me.

Wearing a watch is like carrying a personal coach on our arm. It tells instantly and exactly how we've performed, then lets us save and savor that time until the next run.

But timing this precise and permanent can also have negative side effects. It can exaggerate the value of minutes and seconds, and can trap us in a no-win race against time.

We enter this race when every run covers a known distance, every one is timed, and every workout becomes an attempt at a record. The faster we run, the harder we must run to improve by ever-smaller amounts—until time finally beats us.

Yet speed is the main payoff in shorter, faster runs. Speed in terms of pace per mile. Pace as captured on the watch for a known distance.

Left unmeasured and untimed, the faster runs seem to be efforts unrewarded. So the old racing-against-time problem can still resurface on the faster days.

I fell back into that trap. I slipped from casual to exact timing, from ignoring to recording splits, and from forgetting this final time to comparing it with all others.

Within a couple of months, my pace improved by a minute per mile. But my discomfort and frustration increased just as quickly—to unacceptable levels.

I didn't need to stop running fast, didn't even need to stop taking times. Three simple adjustments in the timing would do.

1. *Grab the time from a running watch.* Don't take a separate time for the fast mile, but simply pluck it out of the overall total for the day—including warm-up and cool-down.

   Timing the mile this way makes it a more normal part of the day's run, most of which remains unchecked for pace. It also reminds me that this isn't a true race because the time for the fast portion is inexact.

2. *Take no splits.* Don't let them divert attention from where it belongs—on holding a constant effort instead of a steady pace.

The proper fast effort is what feels right, not what a watch says is right. That effort rides the borderline between hard enough and too hard. The pace where that line appears will vary not only from day to day but from minute to minute.

3. *Check only the final time.* Let it come as both a surprise and a prize.

I'm surprised at the time because I haven't paid it any attention until now. If the effort felt right, any time will be rewarding.

This prize flashes briefly across the watch, just long enough for a rough calculation of pace, then it's gone as the day's run continues with a cool-down. A running watch makes this moment more precious by showing how fleeting it is.

Concentrate on running smoothly and strongly during faster efforts, not on your split times.

Truer Paces

Writing takes weeks to travel through printing presses and post offices, and then more time passes before responses from readers come back to me. By then, the passions that sparked both the story and the replies have cooled.

I like speaking my advice to groups of runners because the feedback is instantaneous. No sooner did I make my standard pitch for walking breaks to a group in training for a marathon than a woman in the audience shouted out, "That's cheating!"

She didn't dismiss the walking itself. Although she didn't admit to taking any herself, she said that friends of hers mixed walks into their runs and had success stories to tell.

The woman called me a cheat (she smiled as she said it) for confessing to another walk-related practice. I'd said, "If you ask the time of my last marathon, I'll tell you I *ran* 3:50. I *walked* another 25 minutes along the way, but that time doesn't count."

I didn't time the walking breaks there or anywhere else they had come into play. Digital wristwatch technology let me punch out when stopping and back in when resuming running. The pauses for walks went unrecorded, as if they didn't exist.

I took the opposite view from my smiling critic. Putting any nonrunning into my logbook would have seemed like cheating.

But is it? This woman tweaked my conscience.

Maybe I wasn't cheating by walking, but was it lying to say I'd *run* a marathon this way? The running really amounted to only 24 or 25 miles.

The woman also made me wonder if I was being unfaithful to this practice that served me so well by pretending it didn't exist. How could I—in the name of all that was honest, accurate, and simple—keep ignoring these precious minutes?

Honesty would be not acting ashamed of my walks. They're an interest-bearing investment that lets me run farther, faster, and fresher. So why not haul them out of their dark corner and grant them full recognition?

Accuracy is not pretending to make time stand still by punching a button. Time never really stops. Counting it all would tell me exactly how long I was out that day.

Simplicity is not repeatedly flipping the watch off and on. This promotes clock-watching. By figuring into the total every step run *and* walked, all I'd need to check would be the start and finish times.

The friendly critic won me over to her view that every step counts. The watch now keeps running through the walking breaks.

The amount of walking we're talking about here is trivial. After recent marathons, I compared the run-only time with the official one on the finish-line clock. The difference was about one minute per mile, or less than 10 percent of the total time.

The walks averaged only 100 yards or so per mile. That's less than one and a half miles total walking over the length of a marathon.

The walking amounts may be trivial. But "To walk or not to walk?" isn't a small question. To my battle-scarred feet and legs, these breaks make all the difference between running long or not.

The walks have let me complete two marathons each year since coming out of what I'd imagined to be permanent retirement from this event. I probably never would have *run* any of these events. My run-down feet and legs wouldn't have allowed me to do the needed training or to go the race distance nonstop.

Walking is wonderful. It works minor miracles. It has long deserved, and now finally receives, full credit for all the extra running it lets me do. Doing it isn't cheating, and neither is counting it.

Record Paces

The time was the mid-1960s. Arthur Lydiard was leading the great exodus away from track intervals to road mileage, and I joined it.

Along with many other converts, I misread Lydiard and broke his train-don't-strain rule. I made the mistake of keeping a record time for each road course and trying to break it with each running.

Records fell easily at first, and this was exciting. But it soon became harder and harder to lower times by less and less.

Training became as exhausting as racing, and a lot less exciting. This struggle led to slower runs and to dejection as I ran out of room to improve. To restore energy and enthusiasm, I had to ease the pressures of time in ways outlined in this chapter.

The same story is now being replayed in a much bigger arena. The sport as a whole is running out of room to improve and is starting to suffer for it. The quality of competition, the variety of races, and the longevity of runners all are being hurt by an obsession with the stopwatch.

Race Quality. Winning a race isn't enough any more. The winner must run fast or be judged a failure.

Headlines read "Morcelli Fails in Record Bid" or "Chinese Women Fail to Break 2:20." Using records as the only standard for success, 99.9 percent of races are doomed to failure.

Race promoters try to improve the odds of success by decreasing the competition. On the European track circuit, they pay the stars huge appearance fees to run time-trials. The best runners aren't invited, because that would lead to tactical racing, which would slow the time. Rabbits are paid to sacrifice themselves in the name of world-record paces.

Solution: Force a return to real racing. Do away with appearance fees, and make runners earn prize money by beating other runners. Base year-end rankings solely on head-to-head results.

Course Variety. Keeping official American road records and quoting unofficial world marks have flattened out road racing. The emphasis on setting PRs has made "flat and fast" the most popular buzzphrase in race advertising.

When Juma Ikangaa set the New York City Marathon course record of 2:08:01, commentators noted that his time might have been worth a world record on an easier course. Maybe so, but they also gave an unspoken warning: If you're going for time, don't run this course. If trying for records, don't run any course with hills, with overpasses, with potholes, with lots of turns.

New York can get by without records. But smaller races with courses branded "slow" may not survive.

The demand for better-than-flat courses will grow as long we give any credence to "records" from downhill races. The official record keepers don't accept such times, but this won't stop runners, race directors, and reporters from quoting them as valid.

Solution: Give more emphasis to breaking *course* records, and less to breaking American and world marks.

Runner Longevity. Every runner can expect to improve for many years. But everyone also slows down eventually.

Then what? Runners who take their times too seriously may face a crisis when they stop improving. They may see no reason to go on racing.

Solution: Don't stop timing the races, but also don't make time the only—or even the major—measure of success.

Older runners have learned this survival lesson best. "Runners who focus only on time do themselves an injustice," said 70-year-old John Gilmour of Australia after winning five races at the World Veterans Championships.

Time your races accurately. But don't let comparisons with old PRs keep you from enjoying present achievements.

After quoting Gilmour, Hal Higdon added that for longtime runners "comparing this year's times, whether in training or races, with last year's becomes a downer. An athlete who attempts to match previous workouts on the watch is doomed to inevitable disappointment and, more to the point, risks overtraining resulting in injury. By taking the emphasis off the clock [in races], masters focus on their present rather than their past achievements."

9

Better

Distances

Almost 30 years ago, I started running what would come to be known as "LSD"—long, slow distance. It didn't carry that name then and doesn't need it anymore.

I would have let its 25th anniversary pass without comment. Then a letter came from a Phoenix man named Donald Lakey. He said he'd coined the term and demanded belated credit for it.

He can have it. I never claimed originality; I first read of it in Browning Ross's *Long Distance Log* and don't remember hearing Lakey's name until many years later. I never wanted to be known as "Mr. LSD," never felt much need to defend the practices that became far different—longer, slower runs, and more total distance—than I ever employed or recommended.

A longtime coach cornered me at a dinner and told his LSD horror story. Time had softened his complaints into humor.

"Our whole team tried running your way one year," the coach said. "Hey, it worked. Everyone raced long and slow!"

I just laughed and went back to eating, without arguing. No one knows better than I the good uses and potential abuses of this system, having felt both myself. I know what it can and can't do.

The only personal proof needed for its value is that it has lasted this long. Prolonging my running life, which was then threatened by overspeeding, was the only reason for shifting gears in 1966.

Avoid "LSD" if it means too-long runs, too-slow runs, and too much total distance. Moderate distances as well as speeds.

To my great surprise, my racing times immediately improved after the training slowdown, and they kept getting better for several more years. That bonus led me to write the booklet *LSD: The Humane Way to Train* in 1969.

What I've learned after thinking I knew everything about this subject would fill a volume twice the old one's size. The three main lessons are these:

1. *Regular racing makes this method work.* My results closely paralleled the amount of short racing being done. Too little of it left me sluggish from lack of intense work, yet too much of it left me tired and sore. The trick is to find the dose that sharpens without injuring.

2. *Faster runners need less speed.* I was brought up on speed, racing on the track hundreds of times and training thousands more before escaping to the roads. Once learned, the techniques of running fast are never forgotten. But a runner well-schooled in speed, rather than most of today's graduates from jogging who aren't, has to work much more extensively and specifically to develop these LSD techniques.

3. *This is a recovery system.* My times didn't improve because of any magic inherent in longer, slower miles. This way of running simply allowed the recovery between races that speedwork hadn't. "Junk miles," the ones that don't seem long or fast enough to count as training, ease the pains of one race while building en-

ergy and enthusiasm for the next. Too many of these slow miles reverse the effect.

When "LSD" comes to stand for "too much, too slowly," the title has outlived its value.

"Junk" Distance

I'm not about to pick a fight with my friend and mentor George Sheehan, especially now that he's not here to defend himself. It's not that one of us is right and the other wrong. We merely disagree because we came to this point of contention from opposite directions.

George was first a racer. His training had to answer the question, "How does it contribute to my racing?"

I haven't trained specifically for racing in nearly 30 years. The best test question for my running is, "How well does it last?"

During an interview, George spoke rather harshly of long, slow, distance running. I have some vested interest in LSD as the writer of a booklet that praised it.

"LSD was a bad idea," said George in a *Masterpieces* magazine article by Jerry Morrison. "It produced junk miles, took a lot of time from the family, and actually caused a loss of speed.

"Runners are doing less now—most under 50 miles per week and some under 35 miles. Believe it or not, they are racing better."

I conceded that George was right from his point of view. LSD isn't the most efficient way to train for races.

> Match your maximum training distance to the length of your longest race. But run it slower than race pace.

I didn't question his premise but only his choice of words. One word, really—the one widely and disparagingly applied to slower, easier mileage: "junk."

George Sheehan knew, of course, what others still need to recognize: that many runners run for reasons besides racing. Purposes like relaxation, recreation, and meditation aren't best served by short distances and fast paces, but by running longer and more slowly.

My switch to LSD began in 1966. I didn't make this change for racing's sake, and in fact thought I'd retired from racing.

"My racing times had sunk to terrible levels, from a peak mile of 4:18 two years earlier to a most recent 4:44," I wrote in the booklet. "And when training is as unpleasant as mine was at the moment, only good racing times could compensate."

I came to LSD with "low aims and no illusions." My main interest was "finding an immediate way to make this training business a little less painful."

"Business" was what training was then—a job. It became a vacation by comparison.

My racing didn't end. Some best-ever times followed.

Where LSD worked its real magic, though, was in everyday running. Before, I'd seen nothing but the moving hand of the pre-digital stopwatch. I'd focused on nothing but beating the clock that stood at the end of each run as sole judge of its worth.

Slowing down let me know where I was going and what was going on there. It let me see, hear, talk, and think. It let me put words into my diary and not just numbers.

George Sheehan's statement about LSD used the past tense, as if it were a dead practice. It's still very much alive for me. It has passed my test for any technique by lasting for all these years with few revisions.

The main difference is in racing, which I rarely do anymore and don't miss. The main danger of LSD, warned the 1969 booklet, is that it could become an end in itself.

"LSD opens a new, big, and pleasant world outside of the competitive one," I wrote then. "Living in that one alone can be fulfilling enough. But is that so bad?"

Ninety-nine percent of the running I've done since 1966 has made no direct contribution to racing success. But I'd call less than one percent of those miles "junk."

Minimum Distance

Warren Finke, codirector of the Portland Marathon Clinic, stood before his pupils two months prior to the race. I was to speak next.

"Is there anyone here who hasn't yet run 20 miles?" he asked. I was one of the few to hold up a hand.

"You don't count," Warren told me. He knew my marathon approach and had asked me not to talk much about it here, for fear of contradicting these teachers and confusing these students.

I wasn't running the Portland Marathon that year but had entered New York City's scheduled for a month later. I wouldn't go anywhere near 20 miles beforehand and hadn't gone that far in more than 20 years.

"I don't recommend this if it's your first marathon or if you want to set a PR," I told this group. "But I'm trying to perfect the no-training marathon program."

I added that my marathons are now survival tests. "I want to do the least preparation needed to survive the distance. That's little more than I'd be doing routinely anyway."

© Photo Run/Victor Sailer

George Sheehan ran shorter distances throughout his long running life.

"No-training" doesn't mean not running. I run regularly, of course, but just don't make the special efforts—such as 20-mile and even longer runs—that are the centerpiece of most marathon programs.

George Sheehan told me this was okay. He ran 30 miles—total—in a good week, going up to 10 miles twice and racing on the weekend. This minimal plan let him run a 3:01 marathon in his early 60s.

"In my early days of running," George wrote, "special training for a marathon was an idea yet to come. The marathon was a race like our other races—longer, of course, but except for Boston no big deal."

He didn't follow the crowd as training became more specialized and sophisticated. But he noticed that his friends changed as marathons approached.

They would tell him, "I can't race this weekend. I have to get in my long run."

George kept racing his 10-milers and racing often. If he ran longer than 10, it was in a race.

"High mileage is thought to ensure finishing a marathon," he said. "The truth is that pace, not training mileage, is the crucial element to success in marathons. Witness elite runners training 140 miles a week who are unable to finish.

"I found I could run a respectable marathon on 30 miles per week. I also figured out by observing my colleagues that if I doubled my miles on the roads, I could probably improve my marathon time by five minutes. In return I would risk the staleness, illness, and injury that come with excessive mileage."

Make your long run the most important feature of marathon training. De-emphasize total weekly mileage.

Like many of the good lessons in running, this one came to me by accident. I stumbled onto it after a dozen years of training for marathons the "right" way.

I'd run nothing longer than 10 miles all of one year while focusing on short races. Late that year, I entered a marathon on a whim and too late to train. It wasn't fast, but neither was it any harder than before.

I suspect that much of my past training had been too long, too fast, too frequent, and too late. I would reach the starting line already needing to recover.

I'm now down to doing monthly two-hour (about half-marathon) runs at longest. These aren't really training but fit into my routine whether a marathon looms ahead or not. Stopping this short leaves me eager to explore the great beyond on raceday.

My marathons aren't really races anymore. They're survival tests. It's nice to know I don't need to pass tests repeatedly in practice but only on the one day when it counts.

Honest Distance

Word of my upcoming marathon came up in a conversation with friends. "You're running another one so soon!" said Marilyn. "Why?"

"It's been almost six months," I told her. "It's time to try again."

She repeated her question: "Why?"

Marilyn does some running herself. She hasn't run a marathon, but has suffered along in support of her husband Jeff's one attempt. He drew a hot day and waded through waves of nausea to finish.

Their view of the marathon is like the Japanese view of Mount Fuji: He who climbs it once is a hero. He who climbs it more than once is a fool.

I kept coming back. Why?

The best answer I could think to give Marilyn was, "It keeps me honest." Honest with audiences, honest to myself.

For years, I spoke to marathon training groups in Long Beach, Los Angeles, and Portland. I told them how they could train without quitting their regular jobs and abandoning their families, and how they could finish without destroying their will to run again.

> Recover for two to four weeks between long runs. As their distance increases, cut the length of other runs.

I gave runners this advice but didn't take it myself. Seeing so many of them succeed finally convinced me to try marathons again after a lapse of almost a decade.

Marathon Phase II has a much different look from Phase I. Before, the idea was to train as hard and to race as fast as possible.

Now the idea is to get by on the least preparation possible. Marathons are much slower in Phase II but also are far more humane than before.

My monthly two-hour runs aren't really training. They are tests to see if all the systems (feet, legs, shoes, clothes, drinks) are working well enough to justify my mailing in an entry form.

My approach to the marathon has changed dramatically with the phases. But the marathon itself hasn't changed much. As always, it divides into three parts:

- *First part: the ragged start*. Feeling tight and tired. Wondering, "How will I ever get to the end if I'm feeling like this already?" Knowing better than to take these signs seriously.

- *Second part: the smooth middle*. Warmed up now and well into the rhythm. Thinking, "Hey, what's so tough about running a marathon?" Imagining, "I could go on like this forever!" Knowing that "forever" can't last much longer than an hour.

- *Third part: the tough finish*. Getting down to the real running. Realizing, "This is hard and getting harder each mile." Promising, "I'll do whatever it takes to reach the end."

Both the reality and the magic of the marathon lie in this third part of the event. It's the distance beyond my normal stopping point, the zone I shouldn't be prepared to cross.

I've practiced little more than half the marathon distance. Now I must trust the magic of the day to carry me the rest of the way.

The runners running, the spectators cheering, the timers reading, the drink-servers serving, the bands playing—all of this works its magic. But only to a degree.

Magic doesn't pick up leaden feet or bend rusty knees in the last miles of a marathon. I have to do that myself. Running doesn't get any more honest than this.

10

Better

Courses

Jim Dwight was at work on a story for the *Detroit Free Press* about the race that his paper sponsors. The course would be new that year, and Dwight called to ask, "What makes a good course?"

"My answer is different from one you'd get from a serious racer," I said. "It's different than mine would have been when I raced seriously."

Racers' overriding concern is with spending the least possible time on the course. They ask only, "Is it flat and fast?" Scenery, what scenery? They focus only on their watches, and on the backs of the people in front of them and the finish line.

Slower runners have more time to look around. Theirs is more a tour than a race. They ask of the course, "Is it scenic, quiet, and safe?" They often prefer a course with some hills and turns over an unvaried one.

What's a good course? It's easier for me to say what isn't. My answer to that hasn't changed over the years.

A bad course finishes uphill, as Barcelona's Olympic Marathon did and as the proposed route for the Atlanta Games does. Hilltop (they called it a "mountain" in Spain) stadiums dictate these layouts that leave a dreadful last impression of the race. All marathons feel as if they're uphill at the end without making them literally so.

A bad course makes you pass the finish line before you're finished. This happens on lap courses, and on those with double out-and-back, figure-eight, and cloverleaf designs. They make you want to stop before you're done.

The first marathon I ever quit early allowed me to see runners finishing when my race still had a 10K loop to go. I couldn't face the extra distance.

A bad course shows too much of itself. On long, straight stretches without hills or turns, runners string out ahead of you to the horizon. Landmarks at the end seem to grow no closer, giving the sense that you're going nowhere.

The opposite type of course, one with too many loops and turns, can also be bothersome. It leaves you with no clear mental picture of where you are and where you're going.

Point-to-point courses, of which Boston's marathon is the prototype, are both good and bad. Good because they give the great sense of progressing with each step from Point A to Point Z. Bad because transporting runners and their gear from one end to the other can be a logistical nightmare.

Also these one-directional courses can give false readings of time. Slopes down or up, and winds tail or head, make times appear faster or slower than they'd be with equal effort on a neutral course.

So what's best? Best for the officials who must keep these events manageable, and for the runner's psyche and performance?

Map out a variety of training courses. For practical reasons, make most of them single-loop and out-and-back.

Two types of courses best fit those needs. Both use a single start-finish line, just as you do each day when running from home because it's the most handy way.

The first of these courses is the great-circle route. One big loop never repeats itself, giving it the point-to-point's advantages (all-new scenery) without the drawbacks (excessive assistance from downhills or penalties from uphills).

All factors considered, though, the best course design of all is out-and-back. It goes to a turnaround point and then reverses direction. It equalizes the uphill and downhill running. It ties up only half as many streets as the great-circle route (which pleases the local police) and gets double duty from on-course volunteers (who are always in short supply).

Out-and-back courses are my favorite for an even better reason. They let all of us in the race see one another as our paths cross. We give and receive cheers to and from the people who know our work the best.

Street Courses

Paul Reese is a decorated veteran of combat who thought he'd won the fight for his life decades earlier. Then he decided to run across the United States at age 73.

Somewhere in Colorado, this new battle peaked. The battlefield was Highway 50. Reese, who faced the lethal weapons unarmed, recalled his evasive action in the book *Ten Million Steps*.

"I rounded a corner on a ledge with a 150- to 200-foot dropoff and absolutely no shoulder, just a foot or so of road edging. The wind was blowing 40 to 50 miles an hour, pushing me all over the road.

"Two semi trucks approached and couldn't move over because cars were in the other lane. I realized that the force of these semis passing by would most likely push me over the dropoff.

"Sizing up the situation, I dove to the edge of the road. The trucks passed so close I could hear the deafening thrump of the tires and feel their warmth."

The major recurring theme of Reese's book wasn't how many miles he covered each day during the 1990 run. It wasn't asking himself, "Can I make it?" It wasn't marveling at the scenic beauty of the country or the friendliness of its people.

He dealt with all these subthemes. But his main day-to-day concern was with claiming a few feet of space at the side of the road and feeling reasonably safe there.

All across America, Paul Reese faced the skirmishes that each of us deals with daily in our hometowns. The streets and highways are a combat zone.

> Run defensively on the roads. Assume
> that all drivers might run you down,
> then take precautions to avoid trouble.

Drivers don't see us as rightfully sharing the road. They don't even see us as trespassers on it.

They don't really see us at all. That's the problem.

We're like trees and houses that drivers pass by without noticing. But we see them when they think no one's watching and the rules of the road are theirs to break.

On the empty streets, we see drivers at their worst. They rub sleep from their eyes while trying to harness hundreds of horsepower of potential mayhem. They think about what happened last night or what will happen today, everything but what's happening here and now.

We see women making up their faces while driving. Men checking for new wrinkles and hair loss in the rearview mirror.

We see drivers with the day's newspaper folded across the steering wheel. Or drivers turning around to buckle up their kids in the backseat while the car rolls on.

Drivers speed, of course. You'd think speed limits were the *slowest* pace they were allowed to travel.

Drivers drive where they don't belong. They cut corners by going a car's width to the left of yellow lines to save a second of travel time. They wander into bike lanes on the right, which serve equally as running lanes.

Drivers turn without signaling. It's too much trouble to reach an inch with an index finger and flick the lever that would tell a mere pedestrian their intentions.

They coast through stoplights and signs, and often make no pretense of slowing down. They're oblivious to the runner or walker or bicyclist who trusts those signals to halt traffic.

How quickly the safety margin between car and unarmed human can close. One morning, I shuffled into an intersection on a green light. From the left on the otherwise empty street came a taxicab at full throttle.

The cabbie saw me too late. His tires screeched and smoked as he slid past the spot with the invisible "X" where I would have been if *my* brakes hadn't worked. Welcome to another day in the combat zone.

Trail Courses

The trails of Eugene, Oregon, were built for runners. They're as near to heaven as you'll come in this lifetime: trails with soft ground that are well separated from the streets.

The five-mile Pre's and mile-long Amazon Trails now attract an equal number of walkers. But bikes, baby-joggers, skateboards, and rollerblades would bog down on the sawdust paths.

Adidas and Nike money made these trails possible in Eugene. You'll probably grow old waiting for anything so perfect for running in your

Vary the terrain on which you run. Find runs that get you away from the busy streets.

town, but prospects for creating off-road pathways nationwide were never better.

You can thank a bicyclist for that. For some reason, bikers wield more political clout than pedestrians do.

They're much better at carving out auto-free zones than we are. Yet we can share in their victories.

The third-best place to run in Eugene is the riverfront bike path. On my trips to Long Beach and Los Angeles, I always run the bike trails that stretch for dozens of miles along the beach. And each summer at Jeff Galloway's Lake Tahoe running camp, I find new extensions to the bike routes.

We need to team up with bicyclists to lobby for more of these paths. Write to local officials, and state and national congresspeople. Ask them to devote a small portion of highway dollars to mini-roads for biking and hiking.

Support also the noble efforts of the Rails to Trails Conservancy, which turns abandoned railroad rights-of-way into trails. My old hometown in Iowa is about as many miles from nowhere as you can get, but it stands beside the former Wabash Railroad pathway stretching from Kansas City to Omaha.

Paul Reese has a dream. It came to him as he ran across the United States. He wrote in his journal of that trip, "What we need, for the health of the country, is a three- to four-foot blacktop trail taking in many of the nation's scenic wonders—a trail that extends from the Pacific to the Atlantic. Ninety percent of it could be along existing highways. It could be labeled as the 'National Fitness Trail,' with every mile marked."

Reese admitted, "Many people would consider the idea of a National Fitness Trail extravagant. But consider that its cost would be minuscule compared to the cost of space programs or social-service programs or drug-abuse programs. Few aspects of national life are more precious than the health of our people."

The fitness issue might not win many votes. But the safety issue grabs the attention of politicians.

During a visit to Cedar Rapids, Iowa, I heard that efforts to extend the city's bikepath system had stalled. They got moving again only after six local cyclists were killed or seriously injured in one year while riding in traffic.

We apparently have an unlikely ally in this effort to create off-road paths. Drivers aren't unsympathetic.

A Louis Harris poll, commissioned by *Runner's World* and *Bicycling* magazines, found that very few of the people questioned would use special exercise pathways themselves. Yet 72 percent supported government action to "make walking, running, and biking a safe and integral part of the area's transportation system." And 59 percent favored public funding of a separate space for us.

Get off the roads whenever possible.
Break away from distracting, risky, and
unfair competition with cars.

Drivers and runners agree on one thing: They don't want us on their roads any more than we want to be there.

Shared Courses

Try to pull the ground out from under a runner, and you'll hear howls of protest. I voiced mine in the 1970s while living in the hill country south of San Francisco, and the alarm sounded there again in the 1990s.

I once helped conduct weekly fun runs in Los Altos Hills, California. A group ran there every Sunday morning, and by 1978 it had grown large enough to interfere with traffic.

Runners three and four abreast on the narrow, winding roads forced drivers to slow, swerve, or stop to avoid accidents. Complaints prompted town leaders to consider limiting running there.

A news item at the time read, "Los Altos Hills could be the first community in the nation to run joggers out of town. An ordinance to be considered by the city council could ban jogging altogether for two or more people running together on any improved roadway."

When the council met to act on this proposal, runners packed the hall. Network TV recorded the debate.

But the matter never came to a vote. Instead the politicians agreed to let the runners go unregulated if we would agree to use the roads in a more orderly and mannerly fashion. This unwritten agreement let the Sunday fun runs continue unmolested. They've now lasted more than 20 years at the same site.

A few miles away, though, echoes of the old problem were heard. Heavily used trails snake through these hills, and runners aren't their only users.

While visiting there one summer, I heard that a new conflict pitted hikers against runners. The walkers complained that the thundering herd was monopolizing the trails.

Like the drivers before them, hikers overreacted to run-ins with a few thoughtless runners and sought restrictions on us all. Like the road runners before them, trail runners interpreted any limit as a threat to ban all running.

As before, public officials tended to view runners as intruders into space intended for other purposes. These trails pass through a regional open-space district, whose board members made comments such as, "Runners are lower-priority users because they are not on the trails to enjoy and observe nature as hikers are."

One board member noted that "runners [had] never been involved in or concerned with trail issues." The threat of having this ground pulled out from under them involved them in a hurry.

Runners in that area formed a committee to fight the action, compromises were reached, and peace was restored. As this area's road runners had done earlier when faced with the loss of running room, the trail runners learned to share space in an orderly and mannerly way.

Out-of-Town Courses

I stepped onto the racing circuit, such as it was then, in the late 1950s and haven't yet wanted to get off. I first traveled it as a runner, later as a writer and speaker.

My hand and mouth now take me places where my feet once did. I no longer travel primarily to run, but still run wherever I travel.

> Keep training while traveling. Use it as a cure for travel fatigue and a way to explore new territory.

A travel writer called me, wanting tips for running the road. She wasn't a runner herself but was married to one.

The first question hinted of a conflict in her family. I could picture Mom and the kids waiting restlessly to visit Walt Disney World until Dad finished his long Saturday run.

"Why do you run while traveling?" asked the writer. "Why not just give yourself a vacation?"

Running *is* a daily mini-vacation for many of us, I told her. We would no more let travel interrupt it than imperfect weather.

If I stopped running during trips, a week each month would sit empty. Unthinkable! Wherever I go, the runs go with me—but not unchanged.

The writer then asked about the changes: "How do you run while traveling?" A long answer to that simple question led to this list of tips:

1. *Prepare for the worst.* Pack for the most extreme weather imaginable. I once arrived in 30-below-zero Chicago with clothes suited only to the rainy chill of Oregon. Another time, I reached a 90-degree beach with only long-sleeved shirts and tights.

2. *Run on local time.* If you are crossing time zones, reset your watch on boarding the plane and start then to operate by the new time. Thinking what time it is back home is confusing at best, depressing at worst. Why spoil a run at sunrise or dusk by imagining the "real" hour to be 2:00 a.m. or 10:00 p.m.?

3. *Run to cure jet lag.* Get the feet back on the ground, and the head caught up with the body, soon after landing in a new place. The running is an antidote to the inertia-induced tiredness of travel, and the activity helps reset the hunger and sleep "clocks." It works in much the same way to correct car lag after long drives.

4. *Ask where not to run.* Don't trust hotel personnel to map a route. If they don't run, they don't think in distances longer than football fields. They do, however, know where it's safe to go or not. At one inner-city hotel, I asked this question of an armed guard at the locked front door. He said, "Nowhere around here."

5. *Run out-and-back courses.* Keep the route simple to keep from getting lost. My first day in a strange place, I run straight out and back on the same street with only its name to memorize. On later days, I'll explore offshoots from this basic course.

6. *Run by the watch, not by the mile.* Forget distances, and train for a period of time—30 minutes, 45 minutes, an hour. Plotting and following a measured course is hard enough at home, and almost impossible on the road. Time eliminates the need for a pre-set route, and the watch provides a form of measurement during the run.

7. *Make time to run.* Protect this part of the normal routine, even when everything else about the day is abnormal. Travel days are my busiest days. Ironically, the press of running business leaves

me little time to run. No one can give me that time except myself.

8. *Loosen up.* Think of your reason for traveling. Mine usually is to be with someone else—to meet with business associates, to see sights with family, to visit friends. I try to adapt my schedule to theirs instead of expecting them to adjust for me.

9. *Lighten up.* Treat travel as a stress. New people, new places, new times and climates are themselves stressful. Light running can relieve it, but heavy training and racing can exaggerate it. My old logbooks are littered with the damage left by trying to work too hard on the road.

10. *Look around.* Sightsee on the run. It beats driving, where scenes blur, and walking, where distances pass more slowly. Not every run brings pleasant surprises, but enough do to keep me looking for more.

11

Better

Seasons

Skilled writer that he is, Hal Higdon makes his points by telling stories. He does that even as he speaks.

His subject in this talk was the weather and how a runner reacts to it. In lesser hands, it could have been a yawner.

Higdon told about an old radio/TV weatherman from Chicago who had come into the business before computers and radar and satellites took over. He didn't place total faith in the high-tech gadgets.

"If all else fails," said the weatherman, "I stick my head out the window. If it comes back wet, I call for rain."

Higdon added that "runners may not understand the science of meteorology, but we know when it's raining." Or snowing or blowing, or getting hotter or colder.

We know because we stick our heads out in all kinds of weather.

Most people don't. They go from climate-controlled house to car to office to store.

They don't spend enough time outside to appreciate the changing weather. Runners learn to live with it, if not actually like it.

I'm a weather fan. To me, the only "bad weather" is the type that never changes.

Change comes more subtly on the West Coast than in the Tornado Alley/Snow Belt (depending on the season) where I grew up. But conditions here aren't as boringly perfect as Elsewherians imagine.

I once wrote a column about adapting to extremes of heat and cold. A reader wondered, "What does someone from out there know about extremes?" He implied that we have a benign climate without real *weather*.

Does rain count? In Oregon, it falls more days than not between November and May. This weather drives fair-weather runners indoors or into depression, but I love splashing through puddles and coming home with mud on my shoes.

Before moving here, I lived on the California coast—where the climate seldom varies from perfection. However, in that state's interior I set PRs for the deepest snow plowed through and the highest temperature sweated out. Those are fond memories.

My coldest run came in Chicago, near Hal Higdon's home base. I woke up to a 25-below-zero reading, chilled to minus-66 by the wind.

I'm weird about wanting to go out in extreme weather, but not stupid. I wore almost everything in my suitcase, took cover from the wind's full force, and never ventured more than a few blocks from safety. But I ran and felt good doing it.

Accept whatever weather blows your way. Take pride in running on days when fair-weather runners stay home.

My record low and high stand 180 degrees and a dozen years apart. For quick changes, however, none match those made one December. Within five days, I ran in tropical heat, monsoonal rain, and a near blizzard.

I flew first into typically Hawaiian weather: sunny, 80 degrees, humid. Fellow weather fan Hal Higdon and I went straight out to run.

On the next evening's news, the weatherman predicted "scattered showers and possible thunderstorms overnight." The sticky air smelled and tasted as I remembered it in Iowa before a storm.

The storm would last three days and cause the Honolulu Marathon to be run in what Kjell-Erik Stahl called "the worst conditions I've ever raced in." The well-traveled Swede's racing has taken him to all the extremes.

I ran early Saturday morning at the storm's peak. Palm fronds lay on the sidewalks. Waves swallowed up Waikiki Beach. Streets were flooded with calf-deep puddles for 100 yards at a stretch.

This run was the highlight of my trip to Hawaii, but this enthusiasm for getting wet wasn't widely shared. Streets that had been crowded with runners and exercise-walkers at this hour the day before were now almost empty.

Two days later, the weather-guesser back in Eugene predicted "a slight chance of light snow." I knew better. I could smell a sure thing coming.

The air recalled winters during college when I shunned the indoor track in favor of outdoor training. I loved plowing the first furrows on Drake Stadium's track, or taking to the streets in spiked shoes on the icy days when no traffic moved.

Only six inches of snow fell in Eugene. This would be a light dusting by Snow Belt standards, but it nearly shut down this city with too few plows.

I put footprints in the new snow, but found little company on the usually well-used running paths. This isn't a smug, look-what-I-did-and-they-didn't boast. It's an invitation to fair-weather runners who hide in these conditions to join me at wallowing contentedly in whatever blows our way.

Hot Seasons

I'm often asked, "Why did you leave the Midwest? Were you trying to escape the cold winters?" I say, "No, to get way away from the hot summers."

I ran away but couldn't hide. The West Coast is climatically mild, if you're only talking about the 100 miles nearest the Pacific. Venture a little farther inland, though, and you'll find weather in the extreme.

The hottest run I've ever taken—at 111 degrees—was in a California desert. The Army Reserve had exiled me there for summer camp, where crossing an asphalt parade ground was like running on a barbecue grill.

I may live in the Far West but don't stay here all the time. My travels take me to the extremes, including a midnight run in Memphis where the temperature still shimmered around 90 and the humidity was thick enough to chew.

My theory, after running in—and from—bad weather for lots of years, is that the extremes aren't the big problem. We run eagerly on these days so we can brag about it later.

The bigger problem is with borderline-bad days. Two Boston Marathons, two years in a row, stand as examples.

The first, the 1970 Run for the Hoses, was the hottest in Boston's long history. The starting-line temperature officially read 97 degrees, but the unshaded road felt much hotter.

We marathoners knew we couldn't run very fast on a day like that, so we forgot about setting PRs and just did the best we could under those conditions. Those of us who were there still brag about challenging that heat and surviving it.

The next year's temperature was 20 degrees lower but still too warm. This borderline-bad day was more troubling than before because it let us hold fast to our goals and pacing schemes—and set us up for almost inevitable disappointment.

Never have I seen so many looks of defeat at a finish line. I wore one of them then and didn't earn any bragging rights for later.

Cold Seasons

One winter in the late 1950s, I gave up basketball—or rather, it gave up on me—and became a year-round runner. I started running in the school gym that winter, but stayed there only as long as it took all that cornering to chew up my feet and threaten me with a permanent shortening of the inside leg.

"Running outside can't be any worse than this," I thought. And it never was.

The worst part of it was dealing with the reactions of schoolmates and townsfolk who viewed training on the streets in any season as bizarre behavior. When I first ventured out there in winter, they voiced concern over my mental health.

Once I was past the stares and comments, the running itself didn't feel at all bad. Oh, the slipping on ice, wading through snow drifts, and training in the dark on roads with buried shoulders wasn't much fun. But those were inconveniences, not discomforts.

Adapt your routine to the extremes of weather. Keep running, but change when, where, and what you run.

The cold of Midwest winters usually felt better than the heat of its summers. That's because the body is a great heater but a poor air-conditioner. The temperature feels 20 or more degrees warmer when we run, making cold days seem warmer and warm ones seem hot.

© Photo Run/Victor Sailer

People ski, ice skate, and snowmobile in the winter; why not run?

As for fears of "freezing the lungs," they're groundless. I've run in minus-double-digit cold without having my air passages turn to popsicles. People ski, both downhill and cross-country, in winter. They ice-skate, ride snowmobiles, even sit and fish. Why not run?

You just accept the fact that the weather won't adapt to you, so you must adapt to it. You adjust how much and how fast you run, where you run, and what you wear.

Miracle fabrics that insulate without adding bulk make winter running more comfortable now than ever before. You stay cozy without looking and feeling like the Pillsbury Doughboy.

One particular winter had been mild through the end of January. The month ended with runners across the country stripping down to shorts and T-shirts.

In Clinton, Iowa, the temperature that week reached the high 60s. Promoters of a 10K race called "B-rrry Scurry" worried that they might be charged with false advertising. I worried about not getting a planned dose of winter reality, something rare for someone now living in the rain belt of Oregon. We fretted for nothing.

Nature has a nice way of balancing the extremes. Within a week, record winter warmth led directly into record cold.

The big chill blew down from Alaska, bringing winter home to Eugene with a thick coating of snow and near-zero cold. The front then rolled out across the country and reached Clinton in time for the B-rrry Scurry to be true to its name.

Race director Bob Miller beamed as he announced a minus-20 windchill reading at starting time. New snow fell onto the several inches already hiding the road. Conditions have never been worse for this race, which uses bad weather as its gimmick.

Still, a record field of 300-plus turned out. No-shows were few and 10 percent of the runners had signed up that same morning, knowing the conditions.

They trained in these conditions. Why not race?

They adapted for the cold, wearing enough face masks to outfit every convenience-store robber in the state. Not many runners dared take off their gloves to punch watches, and the water stop did little business.

The winners ran four minutes slower than usual. The race looked like a scene from *Dr. Zhivago* as runners' masks, eyebrows, mustaches, and beards crusted with ice.

My glasses quickly frosted over, and I stashed them in a pocket. From then on, the ground below and road ahead disappeared in whiteout.

"How far to the finish line?" I asked a man beside me.

"I don't know," he said. "My eyes keep freezing shut."

It was good to know I was still weird enough to enjoy going out in the cold, after all these years. I was even happier to have so much company out there with me.

Changing Seasons

Winter comes early in Alaska. August hadn't ended yet, and already a runner at the camp wondered, "How do I keep up my fitness during the winter?"

She meant her racing fitness. A moderately tough runner can plow through snow, on slick streets, in the extended darkness, while layered in winter clothes. But speedwork is hard to manage under these conditions.

Work harder in the runner-friendly weather of spring and fall—easier in the cold of winter and the heat of summer.

This is when the California dream comes most alive. It's dreaming of running in shorts and singlet all year, of never having a workout stopped, shortened, or slowed by the weather.

Californians enjoy the country's best year-round running conditions: warmer and drier than most states in winter, yet cooler and less humid in summer.

I've had Californians ask me, "How do you run in all that rain up there in Oregon?" I tell them if we weren't willing to run wet, we wouldn't run at all. Chilling winter rains only cause us to wear more clothes and to save the speedwork for better days.

In most states, winter forces runners to slow their training and limit their racing. This is nature's way of protecting us against overdoing.

Regular cycles of fast and slow, hard and easy, are natural and normal. These up-and-down cycles line up pretty well with the warmer and colder seasons of the year.

Few runners, no matter where they live, can stay racing-sharp year-round. If severe weather doesn't make them back off, then exhaustion and injury probably will.

California's runners aren't soft. Just the opposite—they're tempted by their climate to push too hard for too long.

I seldom got hurt while living with the extreme variety of Midwest weather. After moving to California, where racing and the training for it never stopped, I ran myself into an injury every three to six months.

The running conditions might be too perfect there. They might keep the best Californians from peaking at the right time.

Besides the best weather, California has more people, more runners and races, more high schools, colleges, and clubs than any other state. So how many athletes from that state do you think made the World Championships team in 1993, the year the Alaskan camper asked her question?

Of the 23 runners who actually competed in Stuttgart at distances 1,500 meters and up, only one was California-trained. This count compared to a single-state high of six from rainy Oregon (plus two more qualifiers who didn't get to Germany). Fourteen other states—in all regions of the country—contributed to the team. One member lived in England.

Seven U.S. runners placed eighth or better at the World Championships. All but one came from states with harsh winters, and the lone exception (from Tennessee) faced harsh summers.

Mark Plaatjes trained for his marathon victory in Colorado. Marathoner Kim Jones made excursions to that state from her home in eastern Washington.

America's best two-person finish came in the women's 10,000, and both runners came from the Northeast. Lynn Jennings was from New Hampshire and Anne Marie Letko from New Jersey.

Two men placed fifth in their events. Both were Midwesterners, Jim Spivey from Illinois and Mark Croghan from Ohio.

Todd Williams grew up in Michigan. But he trained in steamy Tennessee.

When the Alaskan asked at our running camp how she could stay racing fit in winter, I told her, "You don't. The weather is doing you a favor."

Know that icy winters and steamy summers give you the breaks you need between intense seasons of racing.

12

Better

Speeds

One of my first and best lessons was to use racing as speed training: Save the fastest running for the races, race often, and spend the time between races recovering.

"Training" this way in high school, I ran short-distance times that improved only marginally under more sophisticated practices. In college, I trained fast too often—and often broke down.

A later slowdown in most of my runs led to better health and, again, better racing for a while. The races satisfied my need to speed, and the slower runs met the requirement to recover.

This mix gave me my best racing year ever in 1968 (as noted in chapter 2). That was the year I read George Young's advice on this subject.

Young made his third of four Olympic teams in 1968 and won his only medal, a bronze in the steeplechase, at Mexico City. He said at the time, "There's no better way to get speedwork than running a race.

"You talk of speedwork in terms of interval quarter-miles and all those things. But you don't get the speedwork there that you get in a race."

Trouble was, I then overraced—including 18 races marathon-length and longer, and innumerable shorter ones in a two-year period. This binge did serious damage.

The scars from old mistakes remain with me. My legs are still too fragile to race at the preferred rate of every week or two.

Severely rationing the racing left a big hole in my running for a long time. I missed the social scene at races (which can be sampled without racing) much less than the feeling of going fast.

Too much of anything can cause problems. Too much high speed did damage in my youth, but too much slow distance also became a problem as I aged.

The unvarying diet of distance tightened and deadened my legs. Then if I suddenly made them race at a much faster pace, they couldn't stand the shock and would likely as not be injured in some way.

Use short-distance races as the most effective form of speedwork. For this purpose, run 10K and shorter.

I needed an intermediate form of running, between easy distance and hard racing. Acceptable substitutes, of the types described in this chapter, began to appear.

For a workout to join my routine and stay there, it must promise and deliver more than better racing times. These additions did.

They became a form of stretching. They stretch the stride, the lungs, and even the mind to accept abnormal efforts without rebelling or panicking.

The results defy logic (or at least the version on which I'd built several previous books). Small but regular amounts of faster running not only didn't cause injuries but actually seemed to lower the risk.

Track Speed

It started with a dream. We were vacationing in California, staying just up the street from Palo Alto High School, where I'd long ago spent summer Saturdays racing on the track.

I dreamed of returning to that track and finding it abandoned to weeds. They grabbed at my legs as I tried to retrace old steps there.

The morning after that dream marked the anniversary of the distant day I'd given up track-based training in favor of slower road running. The dream could have stood for letting my speed fall into disrepair.

That morning, I went to the Palo Alto track to see how it really looked. It was weed-free, its sandy surface smooth, its gates open, a track begging to be used again.

Old instincts took over, and I jumped into an impromptu interval session—the first in many years. Never mind that it went in slow motion compared to workouts of old. I felt back home after having been too long away.

Tracks today aren't what they used to be. They're much better now. Surfaces have improved, to be sure. But tracks have changed more substantially than in look and feel. They've also lost much of their old intensity and exclusivity.

Tracks used to be reserved for athletes, and only their serious business was conducted there. But athletes don't spend much time at the track anymore. They've moved their training to the roads and trails—and increasingly to pools, bikes, and the like.

American runner Ceci St. Geme pairs up for a speed workout on the track.

Tracks in enlightened communities like Palo Alto and Eugene now leave their gates unlocked. They mainly attract slow runners and fast walkers, who meet there as much to talk as to exercise.

The seriousness of the track had driven me away before. I returned to find it a friendlier place, a refuge from the sound and fury of the roads.

Track training had taken a friendlier turn, too. It used be as hard as racing but without the race's payoffs.

Dr. Jack Daniels helped take the sting out of speedwork. The physiologist/coach packaged it more attractively in forms he called "tempo runs" and "cruise intervals."

Tempo runs are steady and cruisers are stop-and-go. But neither session is interminably long or intolerably fast.

Daniels's tempo training for the generic road racer follows a 20-20 plan. These runs "should last about 20 minutes and should feel comfortably hard," he said.

"Don't turn them into competitive efforts. Going too fast on a tempo run is no better than going too slow, and neither is as beneficial as running the proper pace."

So what's proper? The second part of the Daniels plan is to run 20 seconds per mile slower than your current 10K race pace.

Say you race at 7:00 miles. You would tempo-train at 7:20s, or run about 11 laps in your 20 minutes.

Run speedwork at the pace of your shortest and fastest race, but at no more than half that racing distance.

Daniels advised running the cruise intervals at or near a 10K race pace. "I generally recommend the one-mile distance but believe that any distance from one-half to two miles would prove equally effective," he said.

He based the amount of interval training on weekly mileage. "The rule of thumb is that cruise intervals should total no more than eight percent of your mileage."

This plan allows a 30-mile-a-week runner about 10 laps of intervals. The weekly session might be five half-miles with brief walks between.

How brief? Daniels recommended pausing only about a minute between runs. If you need a longer break than that, you're running too fast or too much.

I'd read this advice in *Runner's World* just before reaching the track in Palo Alto. The unplanned interval session totaled—what else?—10 laps at 10K race pace.

It felt right at the time. It would feel even better as the distance dropped and the pace increased.

Mile Speed

The best change in my running life came in the 1960s. This was when I purposely and dramatically slowed my running.

The second-best change came exactly 25 years later. This one brought some speed back into my routine.

The first change was a big one, affecting 90 percent or more of my miles. The second change was small, accounting for only a couple of miles each week.

Back when everyone trained too fast, I talked a lot about slowing down. Now, with most runners training too slowly, I talk more about speeding up.

"Running a longer distance is a matter of persistence," I say in my talks. "You just do more of the same.

"But running faster is a matter of form. You run differently as you speed up—getting up off the heels, lifting more with the knees and quads, pumping harder with the arms."

> Increase your speed with as little as 1-1-1: one mile, one day a week, one minute faster than normal training pace.

That form can be learned, I tell the listeners. You can't turn yourself into a Carl Lewis or a "FloJo." But you can teach yourself to run faster.

The slower you are, the less fast running you do, the more stuck you are at one pace, the more quickly you can improve. Then I explain the one-pace-runner syndrome.

"It means you race 5Ks and 10Ks, half-marathons and even

marathons at about the same pace. Your racing pace isn't much different from your training pace."

I quote Walt Stack. The salty San Franciscan once said of his grooved-in pace, "If you dropped me out of an airplane, I'd fall at eight and a half minutes a mile."

The solution? It can be as simple as 1-1-1, I tell these one-pace sufferers.

That's one mile, one day a week, at one minute faster than the pace where they're stuck. I tell them about former victim Marlene Cimons.

Marlene, a reporter for the *Los Angeles Times*, had come to rest at 52 minutes for the 10K. She always finished her races within a few seconds of eight and a half minutes per mile, which also happened to be her training pace.

She tried a version of 1-1-1s for a month. Her 10K time dropped immediately to 48:30.

That's 30 seconds per mile. I can't promise you that kind of improvement. But I can almost guarantee that your pace will drop by at least 10 seconds. That's a minute in a 10K, and most of you would gladly invest a single mile for that.

I've never suffered a full-blown case of one-pace. I've always had the opposite problem: going too fast for my own good.

I'm from the dark ages when everyone started the wrong way. I ran races my first week as a track athlete, and ran little else but fast for the first eight years.

Even after making the big slowdown in the 1960s, I never forgot how to speed up. I'd routinely kick into a gear much faster than normal at races.

Then I'd pay later. This unusual burst of speed would leave me aching or injured.

One reason I added speed three years ago was to prevent this soreness. Regular speeding helped immunize me against the pains of irregular racing.

The best test of any training change is, Do you like it well enough to keep doing it?

My slowdown has lasted since Lyndon Johnson's presidency. Now the speedup is showing itself to be more worthy with each new mile.

Minimum Speed

Published pieces on training can inform and excite you. But they can just as easily depress and repel you.

Consider the *Runner's World* columns titled "My Favorite Workout" and "Training Log." These happen to be two of my favorite features in the magazine, because I like to read the practices of the best runners. This habit traces back to my baptism in running reading with Fred Wilt's classic book, *How They Train*.

Hundred-mile weeks, 20-mile-plus runs, intervals by the dozens— I've read about them all and even tried a few. I've been inspired to think, "Hey, maybe if I do that . . . " I've become depressed thinking, "Ugh, I have to do *that*?"

The problem with most published training profiles is that they describe work that only a minuscule number of readers could or should emulate. These workouts are only possible and productive for runners with abundant time, energy, ambition, and orthopedic tolerance.

While it can be instructive to read about runners who do the most training they can handle, it can also be comforting to hear the flip side of the story: What's the *least* you can possibly do and still produce decent results?

It depends on the result you want. If it's basic aerobic fitness, observe the Kenneth Cooper minimum of two-mile runs three times a week.

George Sheehan ran as much to think as to train. His ideal run lasted "45 minutes to an hour, and very little more. This is the optimum time for creativity and problem-solving." Of this six-mile run, he said, "The first three miles are for my body and the last three for my soul."

I've written about a pair of my minimums: regular half-marathons as training for marathons, and a frequent timed mile for short races.

The image of interval training has suffered because some of its workouts, like 20 quarters with a recovery lap between, seem to last all afternoon. Yet some of the most compact workouts can also be intervals.

One of New Zealand coach Arthur Lydiard's favorite speed sessions was to sprint 50 yards and jog 60 for a mile or two. This workout took little more time than a race of the same distance.

Dick Buerkle, two-time U.S. Olympian in the 5,000, once had the good sense to write that most runners shouldn't copy his interval workouts. Instead he recommended running just four quarter-miles and adding up the total time for that mile (not counting the recovery periods).

Fred Wilt devised a similar workout that was a model of time well spent. Hal Higdon, once coached by Wilt, provided background:

"Fred continued to train at least into his 50s and probably could have won masters titles if he had chosen to compete. I recall visiting him once and going to a high school track near his home, where he demonstrated the perfect quick workout for someone who has minimum time."

It totaled two miles on the track: four laps of warm-up, then four more laps alternating 220 yards fast and 220 slow, with the last half-lap serving as a brief cool-down.

"That gives you an interval workout of 4 × 220," said Higdon. "Then you go home, having spent probably less than 15 minutes. Still makes sense to me."

You can't get something for nothing in running. But you can get a lot for a little.

Racing Speed

Let's call it the "Sheehan System." Dr. George did little of what we think of as training during his extremely active and eminently successful racing career.

Sheehan used his races—most of them short, all of them hard—as speedwork. The best of those races for that purpose might have been a 5K.

Less than 10 years ago, if this distance was offered at all it was as an inferior sideshow—a "fun run" for the unfit and the incompetent. Serious runners entered the real race, the longer one. Now many of these same runners flock to the 5K as an honorable competition in its own right and as speedwork. It's the point of entry into racing for legions of beginners.

> Give special attention to the 5K—the shortest and fastest road race, and a distance that can be run weekly.

In the U.S., the 5K now threatens the 10K's longtime lead as the most popular racing distance. Five kilometers is roughly the length of the 3.5-mile corporate events, which have grown into some of the country's largest events. The burgeoning Runs for the Cure, some with five-figure fields, are 5Ks.

The only mystery in this growth is why we took so long to recognize the 5K as the perfect racing distance. The perfect meeting place for novice and veteran racers. The perfect blending of endurance and speed requirements.

This is our most versatile distance. It fits perfectly into the programs of track (an Olympic men's event for almost a century and a women's starting in 1996), cross-country (the length of the high school nationals for both sexes and the women's NCAA), and now the roads.

The 5K also fits perfectly with a wide variety of training approaches. The distance is a short step up for fitness runners who train on Kenneth Cooper's two- to three-mile runs. And the pace is familiar to serious runners who practice Jack Daniels's tempo runs for a similar time period of about 20 minutes.

The 5K fits neatly into another common formula, Jack Foster's one day of recovery per mile of racing. Runners who like to race a lot can enter 5Ks every weekend while still putting enough easy days in between.

Race directors love the 5K for different reasons. To name two, the running takes only a half hour or so, and the shorter course needs less policing. The race uses fewer officials for briefer periods.

Shorter races also cause more finish-line crowding. But the Fort Edmonton 5K in Canada solved that problem in its first year. It simply divided the men and women into separate races, which combined still took no more time than a 10K.

This race was a hit. Each runner seemed to want to bring two friends the next year.

Still no problem with overcrowding, said director Bill Murray. He would just add divisions, such as masters and kids, as growth required.

This 5K race winds through Fort Edmonton, a slice of the city's history preserved as a park. The race bills itself as "A Run Through Time." Its setting glances back in time, but its distance is forward-looking.

13

Better

Tests

Dick Brown was as nearly invisible as a man six-feet-four could make himself. He sat almost alone in the bleachers at the end of the track farthest from the finish line.

Other coaches prowled the rail, exhorting their athletes to greater efforts. Brown never once left his seat during the meet. He never once shouted.

He didn't chase after his runners. They came to him for encouragement and instruction.

He didn't lecture them when they came. He coached mainly by listening.

His way wouldn't work with a runner who needs a baby-sitter or a whip-cracker. He works best with mature runners who know how to go their own way most of the time, but also when to come to him for guidance.

Dick Brown isn't a traditional coach. Coaching isn't his profession, he serves no school or club, he isn't a distance-running specialist, he does no recruiting, and he holds no regular meetings of his full team at his home base in Eugene, Oregon. His athletes live throughout the western United States.

One of them, Shelly Steely from Albuquerque, had raced poorly a month before the 1992 Olympic Trials. A lesser coach might have thought she wasn't in shape and then piled on more training at this point.

But Brown saw signs that she had already done too much. He ordered five days of rest.

Steely improved her 3,000-meter PR by six seconds while qualifying for the Barcelona Games. She also finished 20 seconds ahead of Mary (Decker) Slaney in the Trials, which put Brown's work into focus.

He had coached Slaney through her most successful period, when she won two gold medals at the 1983 World Championships. She'd stayed injury-free for about three years with Brown but hasn't gone much longer than three months without getting hurt since changing coaches after the 1984 Olympics.

> Read your body "talk": weight, hunger, thirst, fatigue, and—above all—aches and pains.

Meanwhile, Brown's success has continued in a variety of ways—none of which he would have imagined while attending the U.S. Naval Academy. His sport of choice then was basketball (which he still plays recreationally and which his daughter and son played in college).

Dick gradually shifted his coaching attention to our sport. He worked with the Athletics West club for many years, then left in the mid-1980s to complete his doctorate in exercise science and to start two different fitness-related companies.

He invented the AquaJogger water-exercise belt, then sold the rights to another company. He also created the Individual Trainer, a handheld computer that his company markets.

The Trainer evaluates the relative merits of 120 activities and provides personalized training programs. Brown carries many of those data in his head, which may explain why he works so well with such a wide variety of athletes.

Other coaches might claim more Olympians in one sport or one event. But none can match Brown's record as a generalist.

He has sent athletes to the Summer (middle-distance runners and a racewalker), Winter (a cross-country skier), and Disabled Olympics (a swimmer). He has even coached a world champion in jet-ski racing.

Athletes move differently in each sport. Some move better than others within a sport.

But one body reacts to training pretty much the same as does any other. Dick Brown's genius lies in reading those reactions.

CBS Test

Dick Brown admitted to me, as we worked on an earlier Human Kinetics book titled *Fitness Running*, that his most difficult task as a coach of Olympians is persuading them to train easier. But he laughed off the notion that these athletes should never work hard.

"Challenge is necessary for improvement," said Brown. "The idea is to add challenges that the body can handle." He called his approach "CBS—challenging but safe."

Brown the scientist uses the stress-management theories of Dr. Hans Selye to strike a balance between enough training and too much. Brown the inventor devised a point scale for weighing training loads and made these points the brains of his hand-held computer, the Individual Trainer. Brown the coach monitors his runners' body signs for early warnings of trouble.

He traced the development and application of his methods in *Conversations*, a yet-unpublished book of interviews with sports and fitness geniuses. "When I came to Athletics West in 1978," Brown said, "it gave me a perfect opportunity to look at all these athletes and check what they were doing in workouts. That was when I got serious about refining the system that would eventually underlie the Individual Trainer."

He calculated the point levels of the club's marathoners the year they all PRed and ranked among the country's best. They wondered, as runners are tempted to do, "If we ran so well on that much training, couldn't we do better with more?"

They upped their weekly points by 15 percent while preparing for the next marathon. "None of them made it to the race because of one physical problem or another," Brown recalled. "They had all gone past their threshold, to where training was hurting instead of helping them."

He also recounted his experience coaching Mary Slaney. "I knew she ran into trouble when she got above a certain training load. But when I tried to restrain her, she would plead, 'Dick, I'm not training hard enough.'

"Armed with her past training scores, I could say, 'Mary, last year at this time you were doing X points and you ran this fast. Now you're doing more and should be able to run faster.' That calmed her down, and gave her the health and confidence needed to win two races at the 1983 World Championships."

Brown said his guidelines aren't reserved for the elite. "They are applicable to the elderly and the very young, male or female, beginners to veterans."

Mary Slaney set records with the help of coach Dick Brown's challenging but safe practices.

One rule of thumb regulates mileage: "If you do 25 percent of your week's work in one day, you need to follow it with at least one easy day. You're going to be in trouble if you put too many of those hard days together over a period of weeks."

Other rules deal with body readings. "We've all heard the admonition, 'Listen to your body,' " said Brown. "But many active people don't know what to listen for or how to respond. By listening to what the body says and responding to its signals properly, you have a better chance of avoiding illness and injury."

He noted that the most critical signals are heart rate, body weight, and hours slept. "The heart rate being too high in the morning means that you haven't recovered from the previous day's training and your body's still struggling to rebuild. If your body weight goes down too fast, it means you haven't hydrated. If you don't get the sleep you need, you're going to be in trouble whether you're a world-class athlete or a high school kid.

"We've found that when athletes deviate from norms by more than a certain amount, the incidence of injury or illness increases markedly. Those deviations are 10 percent greater than normal morning pulse rate, 3 percent less than normal morning body weight, and 10 percent less than normal hours slept."

If none of those red lights flashes on, said Brown, go ahead and challenge yourself. For one red light, be prepared to cut short the day's workout. For two red lights, plan only to run easily. For three red lights, take the day off.

He listed a final guideline: "When in doubt, be conservative." Tune in to a CBS program—challenging but safe.

Heed warning signs as you plan your running. Learn the difference between innocuous and worrisome signals.

12-Minute Test

Dick Brown's running programs (some of which appear in his book *Fitness Running*) come as close as possible to making a printed schedule work for every reader.

"The programs are as personal as I can make them," he wrote. "They're based on *your* abilities and *your* goals. I start this personalizing by identifying just what those abilities are at the moment and what your goals are for the near future."

Brown starts building a personalized program by asking three questions:

1. *What is your performance level?* He would call most of us "self-competitors." This means we run races to set PRs but not to win prizes. For us, he schedules four to six runs a week, with one or two days being hard so the schedule will meet his "CBS" requirement.

2. *What is your preferred event?* Most of us race mainly in the 5K to half-marathon range. Brown's 10K schedule will prepare us to run reasonably well across that entire range, but to peak at a certain distance we need to follow the program specific to that event. His book gives specifics for races from the mile to the marathon.

3. *What is your maximal oxygen uptake?* Brown bases all timed training runs on this reading. He recommends measuring it with a timed run lasting 12 minutes.

Ah yes, the 12-minute test! What a proud history it has, dating back to 1968. That's the year when Aerobics with a capital "A" was born in the form of Dr. Kenneth Cooper's original book by the same name.

Dr. Cooper's first book was revolutionary when it came out. This best-seller created more new runners than any other single force in running's boom years.

Cooper's program endures because it remains the simplest and soundest statement of what aerobic fitness is. At its heart lies maximal oxygen consumption—how to assess it, improve it, and maintain it.

Cooper gave us a pop-physiology lesson in this concept we now see abbreviated as "$\dot{V}O_2max$." The volume (V) of oxygen (O_2) consumed by a runner at maximum (max) aerobic effort is expressed in milliliters per kilogram of body weight per minute of activity (ml/kg/min).

The higher your reading is, the more efficiently you use oxygen and the faster you can run. The best runners score 70 or above in this trait, while an unfit adult stalls out at 30 or so.

Cooper has always concerned himself with the least-fit adults. While trying out his program, he needed to take $\dot{V}O_2$s on thousands of them but couldn't do that much testing on the treadmill in his small laboratory.

So he set out to find a more practical test. His experiments led to the running track, where he checked how much distance someone could cover within certain time limits.

Cooper wrote in the first aerobics book, "After months of trial and error, varying the times from 6 minutes up to 20, we finally settled on 12 minutes as the best time for our purposes. This field test is surprisingly accurate [compared to treadmill results], easy to administer, and requires no equipment.

"All you need to remember is the time and the distance. We furnish the time—12 minutes. You furnish the distance."

The only problem with Cooper's test was that it forgot the most fit athletes. He set his top rating too low for experienced runners whose distances easily went off his scale.

On the original chart, we could earn an "excellent" rating simply by covering one and three-fourths miles in the dozen minutes for a $\dot{V}O_2$ of 46. That's only a 6:51-mile pace, which doesn't meet our definition of excellent running for a distance this short. (Later versions of this scale eased the requirements even more for older runners and women.)

This isn't a complaint against Cooper. He purposely set his standards low because his focus was on basic fitness, not on making the already fit fitter.

But as trained runners we also need to know our $\dot{V}O_2$s. Now, more than 25 years into the aerobics era, we have a test for the rest of us.

Know your aerobic capacity. Field-test endurance with a 12-minute run for distance.

Dick Brown refined the 12-minute ratings and extended them to the far reaches of aerobic power ($\dot{V}O_2$ of 75). His ratings, reprinted in part here, are the foundation of the programs in his book *Fitness Running*.

Brown wanted us to test our $\dot{V}O_2$ so we could adapt our racing and training to that aerobic capacity. His system works three ways:

1. *As a predictor of race times.* Brown said that knowing the $\dot{V}O_2$ allows accurate estimates of our current potential over a wide range of distances.

2. *As a guide to goal-setting.* Brown said that we can realistically expect to improve by two $\dot{V}O_2$ levels (in the following chart) within a year, provided our training also improves.

3. *As a standard for training.* Brown said that to train safely and productively we must stay within the limits of our current abilities

12-Minute Test

On a standard 440-yard or 400-meter track, count the number of laps (and fractions of laps) you can cover in 12 minutes. Then look up the distance in miles, the per-mile pace, and the equivalent maximal oxygen up-take ($\dot{V}O_2$max) reading in this table. Dick Brown drew lines for four-fitness categories: (1) "superior" with readings of 65 or better, (2) "high" at 50 to 64, (3) "average" at 35 to 49, and (4) "low" at 34 or less.

Laps	Miles (per mile)	$\dot{V}O_2$
5	1.25 (9:36)	31
5 1/4	1.31 (9:07)	33
5 1/2	1.38 (8:42)	35
5 3/4	1.44 (8:20)	37
6	1.50 (8:00)	38
6 1/4	1.56 (7:42)	40
6 1/2	1.63 (7:22)	42
6 3/4	1.69 (7:06)	44
7	1.75 (6:51)	46
7 1/4	1.81 (6:38)	48
7 1/2	1.88 (6:23)	50
7 3/4	1.94 (6:11)	52
8	2.00 (6:00)	54
8 1/4	2.06 (5:50)	56
8 1/2	2.13 (5:38)	58
8 3/4	2.19 (5:29)	60
9	2.25 (5:20)	62
9 1/4	2.31 (5:12)	64
9 1/2	2.38 (5:03)	66
9 3/4	2.44 (4:55)	68
10	2.50 (4:48)	71
10 1/4	2.56 (4:41)	73
10 1/2	2.63 (4:34)	75

and near-future goals. The 12-minute test gives you those $\dot{V}O_2$s from which to start building a better training plan.

One-Mile Test

It doesn't take a four-minute miler to profit from running a single mile. Anyone who runs can do it.

It may take the rest of us much longer than the four-minute runners to cover this distance. But almost anyone can finish it in less than 10 minutes, and learn more from it than any other result could tell in such a short time.

The mile is the most basic yardstick of U.S. runners, as well as one of the best-known standards of the metric world. This is the way we measure speed, the way we mark pace.

The first question a nonrunner might think to ask you is, "How fast can you run a mile?" Everyone has a rough idea what mile times mean, if only to judge how far you miss four minutes.

Mile splits still plot your progress in a race, even when the overall distance is metric. You quote your racing and training results by pace per mile.

Many training programs employ mile intervals. Frank Shorter, Bill Rodgers, and Alberto Salazar all used them as tests of their marathon fitness. Jeff Galloway recommends them in his widely followed marathon-training program.

A single mile or so can also test fitness of runners at all levels of ability. This time forecasts your potential in longer races. For instance, Dick Brown's tables predict that if you run a mile in six minutes, you'll break 20 minutes for a 5K. If you're aiming for a 40-minute 10K, you need about 5:45-mile speed.

Use the result of a one-mile test to estimate your current ability at longer racing distances.

Test yourself. Warm up well, then run a mile for time on a track or a flat, accurately measured stretch of road.

"Start at a pace you can maintain throughout the mile," said Brown. "Increase it slightly in the last one or two minutes [a half-lap to a lap on a standard track]. Aim to feel tired but exhilarated at the finish, not exhausted."

The faster you run the mile, the better your predicted times in longer races. There's no quicker or simpler way to discover your potential than to run a mile.

One-Mile Test

This table equates times in your mile test with probable 5K and 10K race results.

Mile	5K	10K
4:15	14:05	29:20
4:30	14:50	30:50
4:45	15:40	32:30
5:00	16:30	34:20
5:15	17:20	35:55
5:30	18:10	37:40
5:45	19:00	39:30
6:00	19:55	41:30
6:15	20:40	43:00
6:30	21:30	44:40
6:45	22:20	46:20
7:00	23:10	48:15
7:15	24:05	50:10
7:30	24:45	51:20
7:45	25:45	53:35
8:00	26:25	54:50
8:15	27:30	57:20
8:30	28:15	58:45
8:45	29:00	60:15
9:00	29:45	61:50

14

Better

Extras

You could have counted me as a skeptic on the subject of cross-training. I thought runners had been oversold on the crossover benefits of bicycling and swimming.

I said this as a nontriathlete who is unlikely ever to become a triathlete. I'd rather run than substitute. I did something else only when running was impossible.

Before you triathletes rush to the phones and mailboxes with rebuttals, let me hasten to add that I already recognized the triathlon as one of the best things that ever happened to running. If nothing else, it had given runners permission to train differently when we couldn't or wouldn't run.

I appreciated the values of cross-training, but I also recognized its limits. We runners fooled ourselves, I felt, if we thought that anything but running would improve our running.

Swimming made you a better swimmer, biking a better biker. But to become a better runner you had to run, and to race fast you had to train fast.

Training was specific. Apparent improvement through cross-training came mainly from allowing a runner's overtrained legs to recover.

Triathletes were the decathletes of endurance sport. Their mixture of training made them good at everything and great at nothing.

Or so I once thought. Then, faster than you can say "specificity," Erin Baker arrived as a runner.

Baker, from New Zealand, was a past Ironman winner and wife of Scott Molina, also a top triathlete. Molina urged Baker to take on the

© Ken Lee

Erin Baker's cross training as a triathlete has earned her a 2:36.58 marathon.

running specialists that year. She ran a marathon in 2:36:58—one of the fastest times ever for a triathlete, male or female.

Baker hadn't forsaken triathlon training to do this. The same year, she won a world championship in that sport.

Mark Nenow, who then held the world 10K road record, crossed over in the other direction. He wasn't a triathlete and didn't intend to become one, but was forced onto a bike after falling from a ladder and breaking a toe.

For about six weeks, Nenow substituted hard 50-mile rides for his usual runs. His transition back into running was easier and quicker than he had expected.

After a few weeks back on his feet, Nenow showed his old speed and more. He won races on the road and set PRs on the track.

Part of this success came from getting healed, rested, and hungry during his running layoff. But the biking, which builds "speed" muscles out of the quads, surely contributed as well to his fastest time in his shortest racing distance, 3,000 meters.

Cross-training didn't just keep Nenow from losing endurance. It also gave him new strength.

Extra Warm-Up

The worst part of a run is its start. It doesn't feel good or look good.

We begin running with six-inch strides. We're always tight and often sore.

Looking for a quick fix to this condition, we fall prey to the preachers of stretching. Their gospel reads: "Stretch before you run, or you'll suffer."

Their converts precede runs by trying to overturn cars, uproot trees, or push down walls with the most widely practiced stretching exercise. We do this for half a minute and call it a "warm-up."

It might be wasted motion. There is little proof that these pre-run stretches help much either to warm the muscles or to keep them healthy.

New York Times reporter Sandra Blakeslee wrote that stretching "improves range of motion and makes athletes feel better. But it does virtually nothing to prevent injuries."

Blakeslee quoted James A. Schwane, a researcher at the University of Texas at Tyler. "People used to think that muscles were injured because they got inadequate blood flow," he said.

Runners thought that warming up would increase that flow and assumed that stretching was a warm-up exercise. We were wrong on both counts, according to Schwane.

Schwane explained, "It now seems that injury is literally a mechanical trauma to the muscle fibers. There is no evidence that warm-up helps [prevent such trauma]."

In other words, starting cold doesn't cause most of our problems. Mistakes do: running too much, too fast, and too often.

> Warm up for running *by* running, or by walking for a few minutes before starting to run slowly.

Yet runners keep stretching and keep warming up, and we're right to do both. The problem isn't with the acts themselves, but with confusion over their timing and purpose.

We confuse warm-up with flexibility training and try to mix the two. They're different acts with different purposes and results, and are best practiced separately.

Warm-up loosens you *for* running. Stretching loosens you *from* running.

You need to warm up. To see why, try running your first mile of the day fast. The next day, ease into the run and then push the third or fourth mile. Notice how much smoother and faster it was than the first one.

You need as long as a half-hour to get into the flow of a run. You can find this rhythm only by running slowly through the first part.

This warm-up period also serves as a test. "Run as you feel," we're told, but feelings at the start are notorious liars.

They say you're feeling better or worse than you really are. Only after warming up for a mile or two do you know how you truly feel and what you can run that day.

Stretching can't tell you any of this. Nor can it ease you into the rhythm of the run.

Stretching isn't a warm-up act but a corrective exercise. It counteracts the tightening effect of running.

Runners—especially those who always run on smooth, flat ground at a single, slow pace—lose flexibility. A stiff, short, jerky stride is the penalty for running without stretching.

Because the run itself makes you tight, the best time to stretch is *after* running and not before. Stretching makes a better cool-down than a warm-up, a better way of getting over a run than getting into one.

Staying limber is a long-term process. You don't get loose by leaning against a wall, car, or tree once for a few seconds—but by making this and other stretches part of an everyday routine.

Warming up before running and stretching afterward might not prevent any injuries. But if it leads to smoother starts and faster finishes, none of the motion has been wasted.

Extra Stretching

"Maybe I shouldn't say this," said Ken Lee, running photographer extraordinaire and a runner of long experience. "I don't stretch anymore."

He started our run without any of the preliminaries he had once taken. He said, "I've never felt better than since I quit doing stretching exercises."

Lee had endured a long-term calf injury. He reasoned that those muscles were too tight and took all the prescribed exercises to loosen them. Relief came only after he quit stretching.

Could it be? Could the very exercises meant to prevent injuries actually be causing them?

A story in *Running Research News* suggested as much. Editor Owen Anderson reviewed a study by Dr. David Lally of Hawaii, who looked at the stretching habits of 1,500 runners. Those who stretched before they ran were hurt 42 percent *more* often than those who didn't stretch at all.

Does this mean the ritual promoted and practiced so widely for the past 20 years is at least a waste of time, if not harmful? Not really. But like any form of training, it can be misused.

The *RRN* piece stuck to the facts and didn't say why pre-run stretches might increase injury risks. My guess is that overstretching causes minor tears or aggravates existing problems, and then running does further damage.

Another explanation: Stretchers who do nothing more than this now imagine they're warmed up, and then start the run too ambitiously.

How long we stretch might be as important as when we do it. The usual practice of holding stretches for 10 to 30 seconds or more might cancel out most of the supposed benefits.

> Save the stretching for *after* the run,
> when it does the most good as an
> antidote to the tightening that running
> causes.

A *Runner's World* article introducing the "next generation" of stretching dealt so much with rope-aided stretches that you might have missed its key point: how long to stretch.

Meg Waldron wrote, "All muscles have an inherent stretch reflex that's activated after a strong, rapid movement or after two seconds in a stretched position. This stretch reflex causes the muscle to begin a slow contraction. If you continue stretching while your muscle is trying to contract . . . well, it's like a tug-of-war [that] invites muscle damage."

We misread this stretch reflex, thinking the value of these exercises comes after it kicks in. In fact, as the *RW* story said, this is when we cancel the benefits of stretching.

Waldron's sources told us to stretch to the point of "light irritation," to hold that position only until the muscle releases its tension, then to relax before repeating the process as needed. The release occurs in the first two seconds.

Watch a dog or cat stretch as it gets up from a nap. Think of how you take the most satisfying of stretches, a yawn. These exercises last only a couple of seconds. Any more stretching than that at one time could be too much.

Extra Strength

Speed runs in my family; strength doesn't. We Hendersons are built for flight, not fight, and my son Eric regretted that.

He had enough speed to be his school's fastest sprinter. But as an adolescent, he dwelled more on his shortcomings than on his gifts.

"I'm second-worst in my class in the shot put," he announced one day. "The ball is too heavy for me, and I need to build some muscles."

So we bought him a barbell set that we now share. Eric gave me the excuse to start lifting something heavier than a pencil for the first time in 30 years. Dave Prokop stepped in at just the right moment with reasons to push on.

Prokop is a former editor with *Runner's World* as well as with *Muscle and Fitness*. He came from a generation of purist runners.

"They avoided weight training because they thought they'd become muscle-bound hulks overnight," he said. "Back in the 1950s, '60s, and even into the '70s, runners ran, swimmers swam, cyclists cycled, and bodybuilders pumped iron. There wasn't much overlap of these activities.

"But with the flowering of fitness consciousness in the last decade or so, there's been a cross-pollination of information from one activity to another. 'Running, cycling, and swimming? Why not! With some weight training thrown in? Can't hurt.' "

The promise of better race times didn't convince runners to start lifting. "Frankly," said Prokop, "I do not know of any studies that have shown weight training will enable you to run a mile, a 10K, or a marathon faster. But I can list at least five ways in which weight training can help a runner, *any* runner."

Build strength in the muscles that running ignores. Add weight training or related exercises for the upper body.

Heading his list was "prevention and rehabilitation of running injuries. My own proof that weight training could prevent running injuries came in a form that was undeniable. After 5 to 10 years of recurring and assorted injuries and niggling aches and pains, I was able to end that frustrating sequence by embarking on a consistent weight-training program for the legs (primarily calf exercises, which also worked the ligaments and tendons in the ankle and foot). Thanks to this weight training, I've been basically injury-free ever since."

Ah, the magic words: "injury free." They give runners who aren't built for strength a reason to build it.

Extra Biking

It's never too late and I'm never too smart to learn. I went to summer running camp as an instructor and, as usual, did more learning than teaching.

The summer's subject was leg strength, which I've never made any special effort to build. The instructor was Tom Miller, who appeared after another teacher had already broken down my resistance to Miller's lessons.

Gary Moran, an exercise physiologist, had said, "Runners often get hurt because they don't have enough strength in their legs to endure the pounding."

Miller told how to build stronger legs without weights. At his camp in Utah, Miller talked about a technique that goes beyond injury prevention and into performance enhancement.

Miller is a retired Marine officer. He's also *Doctor* Miller, with a Ph.D. in exercise science.

Tom had run about 100 marathons when his son, with little running training, beat him in an uphill race. When Tom asked how this could have happened, the boy credited the mountain biking he did as off-season training for skiing.

"I started doing uphill repeats on a bike, standing up to get more power," said Miller. "My running times immediately improved. A few of the runners I worked with tried this too, and they also got faster."

Miller designed a research project to verify these informal results. He traded road and trail riding for stationary bicycling because the training loads were easier to control while standing still. This type of leg work also was more like the running motion than weight training could be, and it was safer than interval runs would be.

Nineteen runners completed Miller's program, which opened and closed with 10K time trials. The subjects made no change in their routines besides joining Tom for six weekly sessions of standup intervals on the exercise bike.

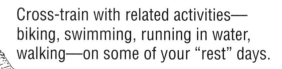

Cross-train with related activities—
biking, swimming, running in water,
walking—on some of your "rest" days.

They sat and pedaled at low flywheel tension to warm up, recover between "runs," and cool down. They cranked up the tension until the wheel would barely turn and then stood for the intervals. They "ran" 30 seconds twice, then two times each for 45 seconds, 60, 45, and 30.

"All 19 of these runners ran faster in the second 10K than in the first," said Miller. "The average improvement was 10 percent, or about four minutes at this distance. Fourteen of them set PRs, even though this was winter and most of them weren't in top racing shape."

The professors who oversaw this project were impressed. They told Miller that the statistical validity of the results was above question and that they'd seen no other study which produced such dramatic improvement in just six weeks.

Tom coaches a training group (the term he prefers over "club" or "team") in Salt Lake City. Two follow-up tests with this group, using 5K times as a gauge, matched the earlier outcome.

"There were PRs all over the place," he said. "One man improved from the 19s into the 17s in just six weeks."

Why do the standing bike intervals work this well? Miller's theory: "They simulate fast running but with higher resistance than most runners can tolerate on the track or road. This training works the muscles as well as uphill sprinting would, but it doesn't tear you apart."

Extra Water

Mary Slaney and I live in the same town, and my rare meetings with her are usually cordial. We once chatted through a cross-country flight, and her exaggerated prima-donna image was nowhere to be seen.

I've glimpsed that side of her only twice, and the setting was the same both times. She was injured and doing water training.

I'd come to the pool to visit her adviser, Dick Brown, and not Mary. But she apparently saw me as a spying reporter, flashed a what-are-you-doing-here scowl and said not so much as "hi."

This was her private training place, and I had invaded it. I learned, while working on a book with Brown, just how valuable a second home this has been for Slaney.

Dick hadn't officially coached her for years. But he still oversaw her frequent rehabilitations in his water-therapy tanks at a Eugene medical center.

Slaney trained there almost daily that summer while recovering from Achilles-tendon surgery. Her history predicted another quick and complete comeback.

Brown had seen this happen before. He began this history lesson in 1983:

"Mary and I had made a deal before the indoor track season that year. At the first sign of any injury trouble, she would end her season. She pulled out in January because of a problem in an ankle."

Eric Bass, inventor of a training tank, read the news. He called Brown and offered to send out from Philadelphia a prototype of the Aqua Ark that Bass later marketed.

"Mary didn't need it by the time it arrived," said Brown. "Her injury had healed, and that year she won the 1,500- and 3,000-meter titles at the World Championships. The tank sat unused in my shed until the next summer.

"Then at the 1984 Olympic Trials, Mary hurt an Achilles tendon. She had warmed up for the 1,500 semifinals, then was held with the other runners in a pen for 45 minutes and her Achilles tightened up."

Slaney qualified for the games but hurt too much to run after the trials. A doctor injected the tendon with saline to break the adhesions, but that procedure only increased the pain.

Brown recalled that "she was walking around like Chester in Gunsmoke. So I pulled the tank out of the shed and put Mary in it.

"She spent the next three weeks in the water, with no land workouts at all. However, she 'ran' the exact workouts in the tank that we had planned for the land—same length [in time], same effort, same periods of work and recovery for her intervals."

One week before the Olympics were to open in Los Angeles, three days after resuming land training, Slaney set a world 2,000-meter record.

"She was more fit then than I had ever seen her," said Brown, "more fit than at the World Championships."

Two days before her Olympic 3,000, Mary finished a fast 400-meter training run and asked her coach, "What was that, about a 59?" It was a 54!

"Unfortunately she fell . . . ," Brown stopped here, because too much has already been said about The Fall.

Remember that Mary Slaney's story didn't end at the Los Angeles Olympics. She climbed back into the water to heal the resulting injury, then got back on her feet later to run faster than ever.

15

Better

Tactics

George Sheehan told in one of his last columns about standing with a college running coach as they watched 10,000 runners pass by in a road race. The coach finally turned to George and said, "This is ridiculous.

"There are only about 100 real runners in the race. The rest should be home watching it on TV."

Before going on to assure other runners that they're real even if they never finish near the top 100, George commented, "I suspect many coaches have this attitude. They want to focus on the best. They do not have time for people who can't make the team."

Remnants of this archaic thinking still exist in coaching. But it isn't the dominant view, if only because so many of today's coaches run themselves—and not often fast.

Pat Connelly represents the majority. As the coach for a team of serious athletes, he wants the best possible results from them. But Connelly also makes time for the slowest runners as the coach for Los Angeles Marathon trainees. His job with the L.A. Road Runners isn't just to teach them how to run the marathon, but first to convince them that they can do it and that doing it is a noble effort.

He must be saying the right things. More than 1,000 people sign up for the training each year.

Before getting into the program, these people have had to fight off the idea that they're too old, too heavy, or too slow to run like this. They had to stop thinking that they should stand aside and watch the real runners perform.

I spoke to one of these groups midway through its training cycle. "Don't look too long and hard at those skinny young speed demons up ahead of you," I said. "Look to them for inspiration, yes, but don't let them make you feel bad."

Some of us are better runners than others. But all of us are good.

For proof of that, stop focusing exclusively on who's ahead of you. For a truer picture of where you stand, turn around and look behind.

Look at all the people there who go more slowly than you do in this race. In particular, look at the people who aren't there. Look at those who began training for this event and didn't get to the starting line. Look at those who say they'll run a race in a "someday" that never comes. Look at those who won't or can't run at all.

"Ninety-eight percent of winning," I told the L.A. marathoners, "is getting to the starting line. The hard part is making the commitment to run and then doing the training.

"You're taking care of that 98 percent now. By completing the final 2 percent on raceday, you'll become a very special person. You'll be the one American in 1,000 who can and will go this far."

This isn't an invitation to look down on the people behind you. It's a plea not to get down on yourself.

Don't disparage your running, no matter what your ability. Resolve never again to say, "I only ran X minutes for X miles," or, "I'm just a jogger."

Folksinger Woody Guthrie once wrote, "I hate a song that makes you think you're born to lose, no good to nobody, no good for nothin' because you're either too young or too old, too fat or too thin, or too ugly, or too this or that. I'm out to sing the songs that'll make you take pride in yourself."

Don't let anyone tell you you're "too this or that" to be a runner.

Take pride in your work. Read the writers, listen to the speakers, and find the coaches who make you feel proud.

Taper Tactics

For too long, runners and running researchers didn't speak the same language. We runners didn't hear or couldn't understand much of what the people in white coats were learning.

Owen Anderson changed all that. No one now writing about running does better at translating technical data from the labs into practical tips for the road than Anderson. An exercise scientist, Anderson publishes the newsletter, *Running Research News* (Box 27041, Lansing, MI 48909), and writes a column for *Runner's World* and a couple of British publications.

Scientists are professional skeptics. Even our most time-honored practices don't escape their scrutiny.

Consider the traditional practices of premarathon tapering and post-race recovery. Anderson dissected them in an article titled "Are You Already 'Damaged Goods' When You Show Up for Your Races?"

He said that most runners take their last long run too close to the event and resume hard running too soon afterward. He quoted research papers as proof that the traditional two-week taper before a marathon and easy month after the race aren't enough.

He reported that Michael J. Warhol's team from Harvard and Tufts Universities had tested 40 marathoners at various intervals after races. Anderson said their leg muscles were in "a state of chaos" the first week after the marathon. The runners claimed to feel okay but were hurting at a microscopic level.

> Allow yourself a post-race recovery period of at least one day for every mile (or kilometer) that you raced.

The damage had begun to clear after a month but was far from complete. Warhol noted that repair work continued for 10 to 12 weeks after the race. This evidence leads Anderson to recommend *three months* of postmarathon recovery.

If a long race causes this much chaos, might training for it also take a bigger toll than imagined? Anderson urged runners to rethink their spacing of the last long run and the race.

He referred to a study by Dutch researcher Harm Kuipers and colleagues. They tested three groups of 23 runners each, each group training and racing at a different level:

- Six months averaging 17 miles a week. Longest run seven and a half miles. Finished with a 15K race.
- Five months averaging 31 miles a week. Longest run 13-1/2 miles. Raced a 25K.
- Seven months averaging 48 miles a week. Longest run 20 miles. Raced a marathon.

Kuipers found no muscle problems in the first group before the 15K race. Eight runners from the second group took these problems into the 25K, and 13 in the third group started the marathon with muscles already damaged.

The damage clearly appears distance-related. It was present in marathoners, said Owen Anderson, "in spite of the fact that the runners had completed a traditional taper just before the marathon, which had included only 12 miles during the last week before the race."

Anderson's advice on tapering? "One *month* of reduced training before a marathon is a pretty reasonable figure."

How much to taper? Anderson echoed Kuipers's finding that "15K runs produced muscle damage in only a small minority of runners, so eight- to nine-mile runs can serve as your longest runs during this one-month period."

Go into your race rested and eager. Train only about half of your normal amount in the final week.

If marathoners need this much taper, why do they allow so little? "Runners are traditionalists," said Anderson. "They tend to do things the way they've always been done."

Runners also are pragmatists who'll adopt whatever works. Give us convincing new information and we'll start a new tradition.

Warm-Up Tactics

July Fourth had barely dawned in Cedar Rapids, Iowa. Already this was one of those steamy Midwest mornings when you can break a sweat just by shaking hands with another early-rising race worker.

The Fifth Season 8K wouldn't start for another hour. But runners were on these streets, doing the strangest thing. They were running.

They would call it "warming up." In fact, this was a reaction to adrenaline poisoning. They couldn't contain their excitement or wait any longer to see if they still remembered how to run.

Adapt your warm-up run to the length of the race—longer before a short one, and shorter before a long one.

These runners weren't elites who treat an 8K as a sprint and need to prepare for its speed. They were typical runners who step up in distance for this event, averaging two or three miles a day and now were "warming up" by running at least that far.

They would squander the reserves needed for a race of twice their normal distance before it even started. They would start tired and finish worse from what amounted to a one-and-a-half- to two-hour workout.

This is so common a mistake that I'm tempted to warn most runners against taking *any* warm-up. I won't go quite that far, but will say that it's better to err on the side of too little than too much.

The shorter and faster your race, the more warm-up you need. You wouldn't dare try to run cold at one or two minutes per mile faster than your everyday pace.

So you run an easy mile or two before the race to find your rhythm. Then you take some stretching and add some striding at the top speed of the race.

This all takes about a half hour, and it's all necessary before short, fast racing. But when the race approaches or exceeds your normal training distance and matches everyday pace (as the events usually do for most of us), then warm-up becomes minimal or even optional.

The longer the race, the colder I start it. I only warm up fully (as described before) for races of 5K and less, take an abbreviated warm-up (maybe just an easy mile) for an 8K or 10K, and do none at all for any race lasting longer than my usual training hour.

In the longer races, I not only want to save the running for when it counts. I also want to guard against starting too fast.

Warming up too well can leave me too loose and eager. It can lead me into an opening pace that I'll regret later.

This is especially true in half-marathons and marathons. Warming up before these events involves no running. It simply means getting out of bed at least an hour before start time, taking a wake-up shower before the race, then walking to the start to work out the worst of the kinks.

My first running steps come at the starting gun. They naturally come haltingly at first.

I don't hurry these steps, but treat the early miles as warm-up time. This is in keeping with advice that Tom Osler gave me long ago for running long races.

"Divide your race into thirds," said Osler, one of running's little-sung geniuses. "Use the first third for warming up, the middle third for doing your strongest racing, and the final third for using whatever you have left."

Better to save for that end than to spend before the start.

Pacing Tactics

Look beyond the questions that surround the world-record-setting women runners from China. Look beneath the unbelievable times of Wang Junxia and Qu Yunxia, and see how those races were run.

Wang Junxia and Qu Yunxia paced their record races in textbook fashion. Their way can serve you just as well in your quest for personal bests.

You know that an even pace is most efficient. But must it be dead even? And must you check it for each lap or mile along the way?

Answering the second question first: No, the only split you really need to remember is your halfway time.

In answer to the other question: No, the splits for each half can vary up to one percent from dead even.

Owen Anderson's *Running Research News* lent support to the 51-49 rule. A study of record-setting races showed that the first half rarely took more than 51 percent or less than 49 percent of the total time.

An opening split above 51 percent puts a runner too far behind schedule to make up all the lost time later. A halfway split below 49 percent sets a runner up to lose too much time later on.

One percent either side of even pace doesn't give much leeway. It's less than five seconds per mile of the race.

So how well did the Chinese world records follow the 51-49 rule? Almost perfectly.

Wang Junxia and Qu Yunxia defied logic with the overall times they ran. But their splits nearly fit the expected pattern.

Wang negative-split both of her record races. The first half of the 10,000 took 51.1 percent of total time, and the first half of the 3,000 took 50.6 percent.

Qu Yunxia—a master of pacing—at the 1992 World Cross Country Championships.

Qu's splits were positive in her 1,500. She ran precise 49.0-51.0 percentages.

The 51-49 rule doesn't just apply to world-beaters. It might mean even more to those of us whose training allows little room for pacing errors and to whom racing times are our main way of winning.

> Aim to run each half of your race in about the same time—and ideally slightly faster in the closing half.

I've run hundreds of races, but only now have I measured any of them to the 51-49 test. The further I strayed from even pace, the worse the result—and vice versa.

My PRs for the 10 most-often-run distances, from mile to marathon, averaged 50.2 percent for the opening half. That's a deviation from even pace of less than one second per mile.

The 51-49 rule can help you in race planning and analysis. Before a race, multiply your time goal by 51 percent and 49 percent.

Say you expect to run a 40-minute 10K. Plan to run the first 5K no slower than 20:24 and no faster than 19:36.

After a race, divide your final time by the halfway split. If you passed 5K in 19:03 on the way to a slower-than-hoped 40:30 finish, you had a faster opening pace—at 47 percent—than you could maintain. Even out the splits next time.

Running even pace doesn't mean that the two halves will feel the same. The second half will always seem faster because you're working harder to hold your pace—and because you're passing all those people who couldn't hold theirs.

Improving your times as you mature as a runner doesn't necessarily require starting faster. Mainly you learn to hold the early pace longer, to spread your effort more evenly over the whole distance, to run the segments at near-equal pace.

Note, for instance, what has happened in the mile as that event has matured. Walter George set the first official record of 4:12.8 in 1886. Noureddine Morceli holds the current mark of 3:44.39.

George took only 48.2 percent of his total time to run his first half, then paid for it with a 51.8-percent finish. Morceli's percentages were 50.1 and 49.9.

The point is this: The closer any time—world record or PR—gets to the best possible, the more even the pacing must be.

16

Better

Races

A friend named Mike called for counseling. He faced a 50-mile run in the next few weeks and wondered if his training would take him that far.

"I haven't trained longer than 20 miles," Mike said. "But I plan to use the two tricks you talk about, the walking breaks and the sugared drinks. Do you think I can finish?"

Sure, I said. He had run many nonstop marathons, so there was no reason to think he couldn't go twice that far interval-style.

Mike wasn't so sure. He's a man of logic, a scientist by training, and this idea of doubling his distance didn't make sense to him.

But no one ever said that racing is logical. It's magical in ways more basic than the effects of the Tom Osler-inspired walking and drinking tricks (which, after all, can work just as well in training).

The race atmosphere itself is magical. It takes you places you could never go alone.

There is no comparison between your routine miles, run in solitude, and your racing miles. On raceday, you feed off the runners around you and the fans along the streets, the bands playing, the splits shouted, the drinks handed.

The resulting adrenaline rush has a measurable effect on distances and times. With me, this effect is totally predictable but no less magical.

In an earlier chapter, I talked of needing only half-marathon training runs to complete marathons. You might wonder, "Where does the other half come from?"

The answer is the raceday magic. It will work if I don't blow the pacing. It will magically double the normal distance that I can run at a certain pace, or it will cut a minute or two per mile from my pace at a certain distance.

Sometimes it has both effects at once. In half-marathons, I've sometimes doubled my scant training distances *and* gone a minute per mile below their pace.

However, don't miss the other half of my point here. Yes, the race is magical. But no, the magic doesn't come without cost.

You can never completely fake a race. You can go well beyond the routine, but your training amounts and paces still set the limits of how much farther or faster you can go. You must maintain at least a nodding acquaintance with race-like efforts.

Trust in the magic of raceday. Assume it will let you dramatically increase normal distance and pace.

Believing in the magic simply relieves you of trying to match the race distance mile for mile and the pace minute for minute in training. You're free to do less work than you might have thought was required.

I train small portions of the race: from a mile at 5K pace to about two hours at marathon pace. Then I trust the raceday effect to do the rest.

One final caution—to friend Mike, to you, and to myself: The magic leaves behind a hangover.

We dig deep into our reserves to go as far and fast as we do. The extra distance and speed leave obvious aftereffects, not the least of them being adrenaline debt. We must recognize the need to take about twice as long to recover from racing as from training. Personally I need to rest for two days after any race and to run easily for one *week* per hour of racing before dipping again into the magical source.

Humbling Races

I can laugh it off now. But at the time it carried the sting of truth that I wasn't yet ready to hear.

It was my first year of writing about running and of running marathons. The course that day was out-and-back. One of the runners, who was well into his trip home, shouted, "If you know so much, why are you so far behind?" I wanted to trip him.

Decades later, a checkpoint timer called out to me at another marathon. "What are you doing way back here?" he asked. "At this rate, you won't even break four hours."

"Good," I responded lightly, "I'm trying for a PW today." A personal worst.

If you want to know the runner you really are, not the one you once were or imagine yourself becoming, run a marathon. Any marathon will do.

This humbler happened to be Avenue of the Giants. It cut me down to size.

The Avenue's course isn't hard, and its weather isn't usually harsh. Even on a rare warm day, giant redwoods shade nine-tenths of the distance. Road signs warn drivers to use headlights all day.

The giant trees seem to shrink you. They've taken as long as 2,000 years to grow as tall as 300 feet. The redwoods are room-sized at their base. They take so long to pass that you seem to run in slow motion. The forest swallows sounds, stilling runners' voices and quieting footfalls.

The Avenue was especially humbling this time. It reminded me that I'm not in final control.

I can choose a marathon wisely and prepare for it well. But I get no say about the raceday that turns up. I must run on nature's terms. Those terms were doubly unsettling here.

Nine days before the race, a 6.9 earthquake shook this area. It caused heavy damage in the town of Ferndale, a marathon's distance from the Avenue.

Aftershocks continued. One big enough to sway redwoods jolted visiting runners awake a day before the marathon.

It's unnerving to think you can't trust the ground to lie still. But at least you could rationalize that the forest might be the safest place during a quake. These trees have stood up to uncounted shakings.

The more immediate concern was heat. The roll of the weather dice brought an 80-degree day, too hot even for the canopy of redwoods to neutralize.

I thought I'd outsmart the heat by slowing down to PW pace and drinking often. Neither trick worked well enough.

I turned into one big cramp in the late miles and walked more often than planned. Pride had been set aside.

A woman and I hopscotched ahead of each other while trading walking breaks. She said, "I see you've become a biathlete too." I laughed.

Later I traded good wishes with another fellow struggler. "Do whatever it takes to finish," I told him.

"And keep doing it for however long it takes," he said. Time was beyond mattering. Finishing was all that counted now.

All three of us finished. The ground didn't heave. The redwoods didn't bow down to us. What we did was important only to us.

My forecast of a PW had come true. But it was a personal worst only by one rather insignificant standard.

Marathoners can say of their finishes what pilots say of their landings. Any you can walk away from is good enough to let you take a small measure of pride along with the big dose of humility.

Today's Races

"Tell us about the major trends you're observing in the sport," said Les Smith while introducing my talk at his Race Directors' Workshop at the Portland Marathon, which he directs. The directors there should have been giving me their observations. They listen to the heartbeat of racing more closely than I do.

I confessed to them, "I haven't directed a race since the mid-1970s. The last one was the worst as I trusted the local police to know their own town. The lead cop took the first 25 runners on a quarter-mile shortcut, and after sorting out the results I lost interest in directing races."

Second confession: "I prefer low-frills or no-frills events with fields that number in the hundreds or dozens to the bigger productions that are the rule today." I cited the Avenue of the Giants as one exception to this rule. It's a throwback to pre-boom times when just about everyone knew everyone who ran, and races resembled family reunions.

Give meaning to your finishing place by calculating it as a percentage of the total number of runners in the race.

But even in the big-numbers game that is road racing today, friendliness is making a strong comeback. No one can know everyone at a race anymore, but runners are carving smaller communities from the crowds. This teaming up is the most exciting current trend at the races.

You see it in the groups that gather to train for marathons. I've spoken to and run with such clinics in several cities. Formal Jeff Galloway-style programs of this sort have sprung up at a dozen different sites, and impromptu training groups exist wherever there is a race.

© Photo Run/Victor Sailer

A race today is as much a social event as it is an athletic one.

Of the four fastest-growing types of races, three involve teams: corporate races, alumni races, and relay races.

Five of the country's 20 largest races are Corporate Cups. They're limited to company teams.

Alamo's Alumni series appeals to the school spirit in older runners. They run as college teams in these races.

The largest race in Oregon is the Hood-to-Coast Relay. One of Canada's biggest is the Jasper-to-Banff Relay.

Marathon-length relays are sprouting everywhere now that this is a World Championship event. Oldest and best-attended of these is the Jimmy Stewart Relay in southern California.

Races promoted family values before that term became politically charged. The Portland Marathon stands as an example of an event that has expanded to involve whole families.

Make running a team and family sport. Join a club or relay team, and involve the whole family on raceday.

Portland has overcome the old problem of family boredom and resentment as Mom held Dad's sweats for three or four hours while trying to keep Junior entertained. Today one parent can run the marathon, another can run or walk five miles, and the kids can enter a race of their own. Everyone stays busy and happy.

Races themselves have become less competitive and more friendly. Fields are aging and mellowing. The percentage of runners and walkers (as opposed to pure PR-chasing racers) is increasing nationwide, and average times are probably slower now than ever before.

The term "race" barely fits most of today's events. They're as much social as athletic.

Astute race directors—notably, those with the New York Road Runners Club—have recognized this by de-emphasizing awards ceremonies in favor of post-race parties. Awards interest a shrinking number of runners, while parties let everyone celebrate with friends and family.

I urged the directors in Portland, "Embrace and promote these family values that have nothing to do with political slogans and everything to do with making running a team sport."

Counting Races

Sy Mah did what I can only dream of doing. The college professor from Ohio reached a goal that makes my mouth water. He ran more than 1,000 races in his career, 524 of them marathons.

This isn't a feat requiring great talent, or even maximum effort in each race. What it mainly takes is time: almost 20 years of weekly races, or longer if the count adds up at a slower rate. (You know by now that I recommend against racing more than once a week, at the cost of essential recovery time.)

Few of today's runners have raced steadily since the 1970s, so the roll of those who've gone to starting lines this often is short. Johnny Kelley, a racer for most of his 80-plus years, reached number 1,000 long ago. George Sheehan never kept count, but he probably averaged a race a week between his mid-40s and his early 70s. But not many other racers are old enough or busy enough to have come close.

If my early pace had held up, I would have passed this milestone at a rather young age. It took me just 15 years to reach 500; then the growth rate slowed. Twenty more years has left me little more than two-thirds of the way to 1,000, which at this pace might have to be an 80th birthday present.

I have many excuses for slowing the count, but losing interest in racing isn't one of them. The ability to race has fallen off dramatically, but the appeal of raceday has stayed constant.

> Take pride in whatever your race experiences might be, knowing that only you could have collected them.

I've never run out of reasons to enter races. First came the joy of simply finishing, then improving times, then winning minor-league races, then improving some more while following the leaders at big-league events.

Improvement eventually stopped, but racing didn't. In the next period, success was measured by effort instead of time. Any race run harder than the daily norms of pace or distance counted as a victory.

Now it counts just to be there at a race. I don't often run all-out anymore because my touchy feet and legs don't like the unpleasant surprises of extraordinary effort. They protest for days or weeks afterward, which interferes with my overriding goal of keeping going as a runner.

I still run in races but seldom *race* them. I don't go to races to run good times but to *have* them. My main reason for going there now is to stay in touch with the sport and its people.

For one who works full-time in running, I have very little direct contact with runners. Daily runs are an extension of writing and must be done alone. I write alone for unseen runners and rarely hear from them. My speeches are monologues, not conversations.

Much of what I read, write, hear, and say has little to do with my own running. My dealings are mostly at the higher levels of the sport, where people seem younger and faster and more professional all the time. Only at the races do I see, talk with, and run beside other ordinary runners.

I once thought the best racing memories would center on fast times and long distances run. They don't. They focus on places traveled and people met. My ability to race fast is gone now. But the best experiences of racing are lasting and always being renewed.

I'd love to pick up the pace of race-counting again. This would not be done to speed my progress toward 1,000. The count is nothing more than a way of keeping score—numerical proof of staying healthy and hungry enough to go back to the starting line again and again.

I don't want to run races just to reach some arbitrary round-number goal in the distant future, but for what each race gives me immediately. It automatically takes me places where I wouldn't otherwise go, and automatically puts me closest to the people most like myself. I can think of no finer way to spend the rest of a running lifetime than at weekly races.

17

Better

Rewards

For a glimpse of what it takes to win an Olympic gold medal and what that prize means to its winner, dial a certain number in the Sacramento area code. Someone there will answer, "10K Gold."

That's the office of Billy Mills, the only American gold medalist at 10,000 meters. His business career now focuses as sharply on that one accomplishment as his running career did on accomplishing it.

"Focus" was and is a big word to Mills. He used it often in a phone conversation about his race at the 1964 Olympics in Tokyo.

Mills said he had no more talent than anyone else in the field. He hadn't won any of his four previous races at the 10,000-meter distance.

He hadn't trained harder than anyone else. Injuries had wiped out "40 percent of my workouts" in the Olympic year.

Mills's strength was his ability to focus on a single goal. He never let distractions and disappointments blur his vision.

"Even though I was hardly running with the Games two years away," said Mills in our phone conversation, "I was formulating a plan. I wrote in my workout book in 1962, 'Gold medal, 10,000-meter run.' I began training in January 1963 with that goal in mind."

He told himself, "I truly am a great distance runner. God has given me the ability. The rest is up to me. *Believe, believe, believe!*"

His belief was tested often in the final year before the Games. During an indoor three-mile race in January 1964, Mills was ordered to drop out after the leader lapped him. When Billy refused, an official shouted, "You're an embarrassment."

Mills's next problem: "I wanted to average 100-mile weeks. This was hard to do with shin splints interfering, so I extended my 'weeks' to 10 days. I added up the best 7 days from those 10. This way, I could keep my mileage up and stay on track mentally while still getting the recovery days that I needed."

Mills placed second to Gerry Lindgren in the Olympic Trials 10,000. Billy ran 29:10 and thought he could have gone at least a second faster for each lap. He wrote then in his logbook, "Gold medal, 10,000-meter run. Time, 28:25."

Ron Clarke of Australia held the world 10,000-meter record at the time, which made him the Olympic favorite. Every day in training, Mills visualized outkicking Clarke on the last lap at the games.

"Then I realized that Clarke might not be the only man there with a lap to go. So I added a mystery man to my mental scenario, and worked on kicking past him, whoever he might be."

Mills wrote in his diary before the race, "My speed is there. Just stay with the leaders for five and a half miles, and then the race begins. *Believe, believe, believe!*"

During the race, Mills almost dropped off the pace a couple of times. "But I hung in there. The reason I didn't quit was that long-term focus on this day, this hour, these minutes and seconds."

The last lap went almost exactly as he had rehearsed it. "I caught Clarke and the 'mystery man,' Mohamed Gammoudi, just as I'd practiced doing it."

Mills had focused on winning in 28:25. He won in 28:24.4.

"From this race," he said much later, "I learned about the height of competition. It wasn't to beat Clarke or Gammoudi, but to reach within the depths of my capabilities and compete against myself to the greatest extent possible.

"That was where my real focus lay. I focused first on Billy Mills and maximizing Billy's own capabilities."

Higher Rewards

Billy Mills took one path, and Frank Shorter quite a different one. Both led to the same result, an Olympic gold medal.

Mills focused all his efforts for two full years on winning the 10,000 at the Tokyo Games. And he won against the longest possible odds.

Two years before Munich, Shorter hadn't even run a marathon. His victory resulted from a long series of short steps toward that goal.

Both runners would agree that you must aim at a distance, a time, a prize beyond your current reach. They disagree on how far beyond.

© Photo Run/Victor Sailer

Frank Shorter took a series of smaller steps toward achieving a larger goal.

Keep your goals challenging but reach-
able, neither too easily met nor beyond
your ability to meet.

Dr. Bruce Ogilvie, a pioneer sports psychologist, favors the Shorter approach. "All things considered," said Ogilvie, "outstanding athletes are at their very best when the odds are slightly against them. Ambitious people derive slight joy, if any, when their ability remains uncontested."

Note that qualifying word "slightly." Ogilvie said that "the level of aspiration must be *slightly* elevated so [athletes] are always striving or reaching—standing on their tiptoes, not off-balance or in fear of stumbling, but with a ready capacity to regain their balance should they overreach their capacity."

Frank Shorter said at the time he qualified for the 1972 Olympic team that such high-level success wasn't what he set out to achieve. It sort of crept up on him.

"If it doesn't, you're going to go through a lot of frustration," said Shorter. "Wanting to be the best in the world when you're a 9- or 10-minute two-miler [as Shorter was through much of his college career] isn't going to do you any good."

Added Jack Bacheler, Shorter's Olympic teammate in 1972, "You have to keep a perspective about your goals. I've never been very goal-oriented, I guess.

"I remember starting out, I just wanted to make the [high school] varsity. After that, I just wanted to run against this guy I didn't like, who happened to be the third man on the team.

"After beating him, I thought, 'Gee, by the state meet it would be kind of neat to be first man.' And after that, 'Gee, I wonder if it would be possible to run in college.' "

And on it went, step by small step, until Bacheler placed ninth in the Olympic Marathon that Shorter won.

Personal Rewards

I'll forgive Bil Gilbert his quirk of spelling his first name without the second "l." He's a longtime writing hero of mine, one who both thinks deeply and writes clearly.

Gilbert once coached an age-group track team, but he rarely wrote later on sports as we know them. His *Sports Illustrated* articles dealt mainly with nature topics. I read them only because he wrote them.

An old article of his made me an admirer forever. In the early 1970s, Gilbert defined three levels of competition: "true sport," which is child's play at any age; "high sport," which is play elevated to an art form; and "big sport," which is playing for pay.

In running terms, true sport is training alone and for our own reasons. High sport is testing our skills at races. Big sport is watching the pros compete.

Gilbert's essay spent little thought on big-time sports. He pictured them as "decreasingly concerned with sport and increasingly show-biz operations [concerned with] commerce and politics." At the same time, he pronounced the other two levels of sports "in as good or better shape than ever."

Gilbert predicted running's future. Twenty years later, true and high sports have blossomed. Big sport has burgeoned, too, but it also is increasingly commercial and political.

A writer with such insight has earned a careful reading now of his *Sports Illustrated* article, "Competition: Is It What Life's All About?" It looked closely at the competitive ethic, and noted its flaws. Gilbert, the naturalist, said first that kill-or-be-killed, survival-of-the-fittest competition isn't the natural force it is cracked up to be.

He wrote, "The win-or-drop-dead model of evolution is at odds with the fact that, through the aeons, life-forms on earth have become increasingly numerous and various. The multitude of species reflects the evolutionary drive to find a small edge—a niche, zoologists call it—that enables creatures to go about their business without always fighting with others with the same appetites."

Runners, too, have become more numerous and various in recent years. This isn't because only the fittest have survived, but because more of us have found our niches.

I'm a survivor, but never have been super-fit or much of a competitor. Years ago, I took a psychological test devised by Dr. Bruce Ogilvie and Dr. Thomas Tutko at San Jose State University.

The fittest, most competitive runners must score well in tough-mindedness (the will to train and race hard) and aggression (the urge to beat other people). I flunked in both areas.

The computer placed me in the bottom 20 percent of athletes for mental toughness. The scorecard called me "tender-minded." In aggressiveness, I fell to the lowest 10 percent. The computer judged me as an "extremely nonaggressive athlete who rarely asserts himself. [He] feels the aggressive elements of sports are unappealing and nonrewarding."

However, I scored near the top in the area of trust. The test showed me as "not inclined to be jealous or suspicious of others."

I don't covet what other runners have or suspect them of trying to take what is mine. Instead of competing for a goal that only one of us can achieve, we can cooperate to accomplish more than any of us could alone.

Take winning personally. Ask how well you did against your expected results, not against the entire field.

"As a practical matter," said Bil Gilbert, "cooperation is the tactic most commonly used to get what we want. Getting what we want by taking it from somebody else in an overt contest is usually, for us as for other species, a last resort. Therefore a good argument can be made that life is mostly about *avoiding* competition."

Instead we seek a niche where we don't have to beat others but only improve ourselves. Said Gilbert, "Humans have long had a high regard for niches, which allow us to occupy positions in which competition is completely eliminated or greatly reduced."

Running offers as many of these niches as there are runners. As a winner (in your niche) you aren't judged by how many people you beat, but by how well you do against one tough-enough competitor: yourself.

Tangible Rewards

Two letter writers, Eugenie Tendrich and Jeffery Klein, knew better than I did what the pressing issue in award giving really is. It isn't the earning power of professionals, which affects only the tiniest minority of runners.

The real issue is the other awards—the medals and such. At today's races, too many runners stand to receive them.

Tendrich's letter ran in *Runner's World*, in response to my column on women's pay. "I rarely enter races where there are financial rewards," she wrote. "But I see exactly the same inequality in the awarding of age-group medals or trophies.

"While I am not a casual runner, neither am I a particularly good one. Nonetheless I frequently win awards simply because so few women in my age group (45-49) show up to race. It seems unfair when men in the same age group turn in extremely competitive performances and have so much less chance of securing tangible awards to show off to the family."

Jeffery Klein talked over the money issue with his training group, which includes two nationally ranked women runners. "We commented on the undeniable similarities with the distribution of age-group awards," he said.

"The gist of my argument is representation. In my hometown, Atlanta, a large percentage of runners entering races are over 35.

"Is it equitable that someone in the 40-44 age group must defeat 100 runners for an award, while someone in the 25-29 age group (mine) needs to defeat only 20 runners for the same award? This discrepancy gets even more perverse when you notice that many of the masters who don't win awards run faster than their younger counterparts who do."

The greatest travesty, said Klein, is "races where more awards were offered in a given age group than there were participants." David Butwin reflected on this problem in a *Sports Illustrated* article.

He told of winning his first trophy—for finishing third of four runners in his division at a New Jersey race. The director ended the awards program by announcing, "If you didn't win a trophy, we have a few extras. So come up and take your pick."

Butwin said this incident reflected "the bronzing of America." He wrote that "jocks of every age and ability are being rewarded as never before—not just with trophies but also plaques, ribbons, and medallions. And not just for winning, but for showing up and being a good sport as well."

Award giving in running has become something of a joke. The more prizes there are, the less each one is worth.

I offer three possible solutions. One is too idealistic to win acceptance, one might be too simple to work, and one makes too much sense to deny.

My radical idea is to do away with all tangible prizes. Let the race be its own reward.

We say "everyone is a winner" just by showing up and doing our best. So why not prove those aren't just empty words?

You say that's fine for survivors of races. But shouldn't the top competitors take home visible winnings?

Okay, then let's reward only the very best. Give gold, silver, and bronze medals to the top women and men overall, and just one medal in each age group.

You say this plan is too limited for some divisions and too lenient for others. Shouldn't races draw qualifying lines based on the number of people per group?

This solution makes the fewest runners unhappy, because it allows for the most awards. Give prizes to no more than 10 percent of entrants in each division. Return the meaning to medaling.

Treat personal-record distances and times, not medals and trophies, as the greatest rewards that a race can give.

Final Rewards

The worst part of most road races starts after the runners finish. It comes during what should be a celebration, but often descends into confusion and confrontation.

At a postmortem breakfast after one recent race, the director's black coffee couldn't wash out the bad taste left by the day's last event. "It all fell apart at the end," he grumbled.

The race itself had gone fine. Conditions had been perfect and times fast. All crowd-control systems had worked as planned.

The race's aftermath had given this director his only problems. Final results were slow to come together. The awards program started late and ended much later, when only the final division's winners were left from the original crowd.

Another race that I attended had initiated a new director with no prior experience of this type. The role came with her job for the sponsoring organization. Her last impression of her first race was of being held captive by complainers.

They shouted, "You forgot to read my name!" And, "I finished ahead of the guy you gave the prize to!" And, "You ignored the corporate division!"

Such cases are the norm at today's road races. Most of them fall down, if not apart, at the end.

Award giving has gotten out of hand. The growing number of categories and their increasing size make many post-race ceremonies last longer than the race they reward.

At best, these programs carry about as much excitement as reciting names from the phone book for an hour. At worst, they spawn conflicts between runners and officials.

Harold Tinsley, past president of the Road Runners' Club of America and member of the RRCA Hall of Fame, is normally the runner's best friend. But he increasingly finds himself lined up against the more vocal and "greedy" (his term) entrants of races he directs.

Tinsley wrote in the *Huntsville Track Club News*, "The greed over awards is the most distressing situation I've encountered in my years of directing races. No matter what, somebody will be dissatisfied with the age groups, duplication of awards, or what the awards are."

He hadn't yet given up directing races. "But I've sure thought a lot about it."

Tinsley called awards "the least important aspect of the race, surely not so critical as to cause all the fuss. After all, age-group and overall awards only affect a small percentage of the participants, yet these frills cause the race director the greatest grief."

An equally small percentage hangs around for awards ceremonies, and then only long enough for these runners to collect their own prizes. Wait out a full ceremony sometime, and note how the crowd shrinks with each passing group.

The majority of runners who don't stand to win anything tangible don't go to awards programs at all. They hear no applause and take home no signed checks, no engraved pieces of metal, wood, or plastic. But they don't go unrewarded. For them, the race is its own reward.

Accept awards gratefully and graciously if they come your way. But remember that the race is its own reward.

Setting a goal, training well, making an honest effort, displaying toughness and smartness, recording a satisfying time—these are the true rewards of racing. They are available to everyone, but like all meaningful prizes they must be earned.

And these victories then must be celebrated with all the other winners. The celebration involves far more people and is a much livelier, happier event than the awards ceremony. So why not make the party the main post-race event?

Don't do away with awards and their awarding, but downplay them. Cut the awards program to reasonable length—say, 5 or 10 minutes—by allowing no oratory and no long lists of names. Announce only the division winners, and call only them to the stage to take their bows as a group.

Let all the other award-winners pick up their prizes at a table off to the side, on their own time, after the celebrating resumes. Don't let the honoring of the few break up the party for all.

III

Healthy and Happy

18

Better

Shoes

You can make a down payment on a car for what some running shoes are costing these days. But most runners of modest needs and means can safely satisfy those needs for $50.

When I mentioned my self-imposed $50 limit in a story, the editor asked, "Don't you mean that's the *lower* limit in price?"

"I never pay more than that," I told her. "And last year, I ran two marathons in these cheap shoes."

They take none of the blame for those being my two slowest marathons. The shoes did their part better than I did mine.

My shoe needs are easily and cheaply met. Any light, cushiony shoe will stand up to my low-mileage and slow-paced run with a mini-body and quiet footplant.

Note here that a cheap shoe isn't the same as a cheap imitation, one of those shoddy lookalikes that runners wear at their peril. Stick with the reputable running brands.

But don't expect to keep up with fashion trends. You won't see the cheapies listed in magazine shoe surveys. They don't come off the top of a company's line but from someplace nearer the bottom. They aren't new to the line but more often are dropping from it in closeout sales. They may not have come from the factory in perfect shape, but with cosmetic flaws that lower the cost.

Jump from one major company to another as you shop for bargains. Your first two loyalties aren't to any shoe brand or model. They're to your left foot and to your right. Whatever works for them is good enough. And these shoes can still cost less than $50.

Why pay more? For safety's sake, you might think. Maybe you buy the idea that the less you pay, the greater your risk of injury.

Podiatrist Joe Ellis surveyed injured runners. "Seventy percent of them blamed their shoes for their mishap," he said.

In fact, Dr. Ellis found that very few of these injuries were tied to inadequate footwear. Most were caused by simple training errors. The big three—too far, too fast, too often—will hurt you no matter what you wear.

Buy lighter and cheaper shoes, not the most you can carry and afford. Buy for function, not for fashion.

Okay, if the injury-proof shoe doesn't exist, then how about one that promises better performance? The search for such a shoe has filled many a closet while emptying many a checking account.

That search for the faster shoe led to the most exotic and expensive product yet. Igor Gamow, a University of Colorado professor, invented Springbocs.

His shoes are named for the springs in their heels. He estimated, conservatively, that these shoes would cut a runner's times by three percent.

That's nine seconds for a five-minute miler, or five and a half minutes for a three-hour marathoner. Gamow said this improvement comes with no apparent increase in effort.

The shoes do the extra work. But the faster ride isn't free.

"The good news is you'll only have to buy one [pair] in a lifetime," reported *USA Today* on this shoe with a replaceable sole. "The bad news is it costs $500."

The worse news, even if these shoes work as advertised, is that they give the time bonus only once. Then you must better the new spring-aided mark with the same shoes. You must earn the next PR the old-fashioned way, through your own better efforts.

Support the inventiveness of shoe designers if you wish. Just don't buy into the seductive idea that you're only as good as the equipment you can afford.

Rotating Shoes

This time, it was the right calf. The time before, it was the left calf. Before that, an Achilles tendon.

Several times a year, something on my feet or legs *would* hurt—a little or a lot, for a few days or many weeks. More often than not, racing would do the hurting—either a race itself or race-like distance or speed training.

Race effort alone wasn't to blame. Shoes played a supporting role— or in this case, *nonsupporting*. Wearing racing shoes meant taking on the most stress with the least support.

The irony here was that the part of running (long and fast work) and the piece of equipment (minimal shoes) that were most likely to cause pain were the ones I least wanted to give up. I thought about the options:

- Maybe compromise by wearing the same pair of shoes for every purpose, every day from their birth to their death.
- Maybe wear the light, flexible, feel-the-earth-beneath-the-feet racing flats in training, and sacrifice padding and stability.
- Maybe wear the sturdier, stiffer, bulkier training shoes in races, and give up the feeling of flying over the ground.

Then Johnny Clark explained that the options need not be this limited. He said we don't have to settle for one shoe all the time in the name of safety, or one pair for training and a second for racing at the risk of injury.

Clark owned two running stores in Las Vegas—each fittingly named "The Running Store." He also was a rather high-mileage trainer who indulged in a race almost every weekend.

"I used to get hurt all time," said Clark when I visited one of his stores. "Then a couple of years ago I started doing something that really seemed to cut down the number of injuries."

Note that he said cut *down*, not out. No one has yet found a way to injury-proof a hard-training racer.

Clark's trick: "I rotate shoes."

The idea is similar to rotating tires on a car to equalize wear—only no one except a race driver moves the tires from wheel to wheel each day. Clark changed his shoes daily.

He reasoned that switching "equalizes the stresses which are slightly different for each model, and even with two pairs of the same model. This seems to keep injuries from creeping up on me."

It is well known that little stresses, repeated a thousand times per mile day after day, can grow into big pains. Rotating shoes never allows one type of stress more than a day at a time to build up.

Rotate shoes—don't wear the same pair for two runs in a row. Ideally make these different models and brands.

Clark carried the rotation scheme to the extreme. "I now have 12 different pairs, and they're numbered," he said, pointing to a "3" inked on the midsoles of the pair he wore that day.

A running-store owner who buys shoes at cost, picks up free samples from the companies, or takes leftovers from his shelves can put a dozen pairs into his rotation. Most of us can't do that—not when their total retail cost might approach $1,000.

But Clark's idea of switching still has merit. And it can be scaled down to the means of runners who buy shoes at full price.

Having only two very different types of shoes, heavier and lighter, and only changing once every few weeks, as I once did, doesn't work. The switch to racing flats is too abrupt and infrequent to allow any adaption to the new stresses.

Instead don't go to either my previous extreme or Johnny Clark's. Put two to four widely varied pairs into the rotation, perhaps spreading the purchases over several months so as not to seem too self-indulgent.

Alternate the shoes from day to day. Note any problems they cause, and if these recur with each use drop this pair from the rotation.

Buying new shoes before old ones wear out may seem like a big and needless expense. But the long-term investment is the same as before.

Each pair of shoes will now last two to four times longer. Costs of multiple shoes will equalize over time, as they equalize the stresses on you.

Modified Shoes

You had to love this cover of *Ultrarunning* magazine. It was an answer to complaints that running has gone too high-tech.

The photo showed two small, dark men running a mountain trail, and you could see by their numbers that they were in a race. Loose, dress-like shirts covered their arms and reached almost to their knees.

They weren't wearing socks or shoes. Laces between the toes and around the ankles held their sandals in place.

The cover didn't say who these men were. Inside, you learned the names of Victoriano Churro and Cerrildo Chacarito.

They finished 1-2 in the Leadville (Colorado) 100-miler. They're Tarahumaras from northern Mexico.

"Although shoes had been provided," wrote Kitty Williams, "they preferred to wear their huaraches—sandals made from tire tread and leather thong." They made new pairs for this race, using tires from the Leadville dump.

The Tarahumaras didn't set off any stampedes to city dumps. They didn't make anyone discard Nikes or Asics.

But these runners reminded us that we need not put our feet entirely into the hands of professional shoemakers. Even without making shoes from scratch, we can make those from the assembly line feel better.

Modify your shoes as needed. Trim away flaws, loosen seams, and replace inserts that might rub your feet raw.

The running Tarahumaras are throwbacks to a time not long ago when runners had to be their own cobblers. Authors Arthur Lydiard, Ron Daws, and Tom Osler all wrote in the 1960s and '70s about how to repair and remodel shoes.

I performed lots of shoe surgery back then. I still do some of it.

My first running shoes were Converse lowcuts. The canvas uppers wore out at the same rate as the rubber bottoms, and they wouldn't have lasted 100 miles without wrappings of athletic tape.

My first real road shoes were New Balances. I carved air holes in the red-leather saddle to let my toes breathe. (Later, while serving briefly in the Army, I dyed these same shoes black to make them less visible while sneaking in forbidden training runs.)

My heels started going bad about the same time shoes began to come with padded heel tabs. Until the quality of these tabs improved, I excised them to stop the irritation.

© Leadville, CO *Herald-Democrat*

Victoriano Churro ran the Leadville, Colorado 100-miler in shoes he made from tire treads and leather thongs.

Shoes gained cushioning and stability in the 1970s, but they also lost flexibility. Back then, I made incisions under the forefoot so the shoe would bend more easily.

I removed and discarded the useless arch cookies . . . upgraded the original insoles, which used to wear out long before the shoe did . . . punched extra lace holes for a tighter hold at the top . . . glue-gunned the heels to extend the productive life of the shoes.

Most of these practices are now stored away as memories. But I still perform a few minor but essential surgeries with an old razor knife.

For reasons too lengthy to mention here, I never wear socks. This removes the security layer that manufacturers expect runners to place between their skins and their shoes.

I feel every seam, fold, stitch, and flaw more than a runner in socks does. So I take care to smooth away the rough spots before they can cause trouble.

Any tight spaces go under the knife as well. No shoe escapes some cutting around the instep and toebox.

Many ultrarunners have told me they slice away most of the shoe material above their toes. They say this keeps their feet cool and gives them room to expand as the miles pile up.

By performing this surgery, these runners take a step in the direction of the Tarahumaras. The Indians simply cut their shoes down to the minimum—strips of rubber for protection and straps to hold the soles in place.

Used-Up Shoes

We went through some trying and satisfying times together, these old shoes and I. We trained for (if my two long runs could be called "training") and ran in (if my run-walk mix qualified as "running") a marathon.

They caused me no foot or leg problems. They were always there when needed, ready to go any distance at any pace at any hour of any day under any weather and any surface conditions.

I valued the support and comfort they gave. But at less than six months of age, they were already elderly. They could no longer keep up with my needs.

It was time for our runs together to end. If I make them sound almost human, or at least like a faithful dog, that's because a runner and his shoes become almost that close. Saying good-bye to an old pair is like parting with a longtime training partner.

My shoes take every step I do. They compensate for the weaknesses that were born into or abused into my feet and legs.

They serve me well, but not for long. The useful life of my shoes is measured in months.

Wearing them any longer than that is risky, and the critical stage of wear comes early for me. My feet and legs tell me when the shoes are ready for retirement.

I'm hypersensitive to heel wear. When as little as a quarter-inch of rubber grinds away there, I start to feel little pains in the Achilles tendon, calf, or kneecap.

That's my warning to change shoes. It usually appears when I break through the tough outsole into the softer underlying cushioning.

This second-degree wear doesn't take very long to appear. Seldom does a pair of my shoes run longer than six months, and between shoe rotating and rest days they touch the road in no more than 100 runs during that period. Their mileage probably totals less than 500. But at the low prices I pay for shoes, that works out to only about 10 cents a mile.

Retire your shoes before their wear becomes troublesome. Replace them when you expose the heel's midsole.

Come retirement day, when their mileage is spent, I don't bronze these shoes, or store them in a closet, or toss them into the garbage. First they semi-retire to casual wear; then when the next pair comes down the line the older shoes move on to other feet.

My used-up shoes don't look too bad. Most of the stains will wash out, and the worst flaws in the uppers are the holes that my little toenails always poke. Other than the second-degree heel wear, the bottoms remain intact.

A friend named Gaston has first shot at the old shoes for his walking and working. An admitted penny-pincher, he views them as gifts from heaven.

Last time we got together, I checked his feet to see which old friends of mine he had on. The color had passed beyond recognition.

I asked him which shoes these were. "My all-time favorites, the purple ones," he said. I'd handed them down to him five years earlier, and he'd squeezed out five more years of active life.

They reminded me of retired racing greyhounds. The racetracks use up these running dogs in a hurry when they're young, then dispose of them when they're no longer of value that way.

Disposing can mean killing, but the more humane option is to adopt out the racers as pets. I don't have the heart to trash my old running shoes, so they now do lighter duty as Gaston's companions.

19

Better

Products

Running sells itself as a low-tech, back-to-nature sport. Yet its major advances over the past 25 years have been largely synthetic.

The running itself remains simple and natural. But its support system leans more heavily than ever toward the artificial.

This isn't a complaint. Products from laboratories have made running faster, safer, easier, and cozier.

In the 1960s, first Tartan from the 3-M labs and then other plastic coatings artificially smoothed and weather-proofed tracks. Times immediately plunged by as much as one second per lap.

At about the same time, shoes with nylon uppers and synthetic cushioning began revolutionizing running. The old, heavy, stiff, leather-and-rubber shoes had limited running mostly to soft surfaces, short distances, and light-weight people. The new shoes opened up road training and racing to everyone.

We soon started stuffing extra support into the shoes. My first orthotics (custom-made inserts) were hard, arch-biting plastic. The current feather-light pair look and feel like styrofoam.

The 1970s brought fabrics that no cotton patch or sheep's back could produce. Polypropylene, Lycra, and Goretex warmed runners in winter, and high-tech shorts and singlets cooled us in summer. The miracle fibers have continued to evolve ever since.

In chapter 8, I praised the modern stopwatch—which acts like a computer on the wrist. Some runners wouldn't leave home without their transistorized, miniaturized Walkman-type headsets.

We have plenty of technology available to us. The question is: How much of it do we really need?

Performance Products

"What do you have against the triathlon?" interviewer Mark Lemmon from the *Ohio Runner* once asked me. He is a runner first but also a practicing triathlete, and had detected a critical tone toward his second sport in my writing.

True, I sometimes point out the excesses of that sport. I said many of the same things about running when it passed through an earlier growth spurt.

The triathlon is repeating our growing pains on its way to maturity, and I simply report them. I have nothing against the triathlon, and certainly nothing against its practitioners.

This endurance sport is a first cousin of ours in its demands and rewards. Most triathletes started as runners and still spend at least one-third of their time running. Our common interests far outweigh our differences.

But we are different in one fundamental way. The triathlon relies increasingly on high-tech equipment, while running remains largely low-tech despite commercial pressures to be otherwise.

Equipment gives runners little or no performance boost. The benefits of what we wear are mainly protective (shoes against the surface, clothes against the weather) and supportive (a watch for keeping score, a headset for entertainment). We still run our fastest while wearing the least that conditions and the law will allow.

Not so in the triathlon. Races favor the athlete who wears the sleekest wetsuit to improve swimming speed or rides the swiftest bicycle.

Equipment choices make vast differences in triathletes' times. This fact has sparked intramural debate over the need to regulate or standardize the tools of that sport.

Triathlon Today editor Lew Kidder wrote that "sometimes startling developments in technology are raising a critical issue for the sport of triathlon. Disk wheels, wheel covers, innovative pedal systems, aerodynamic handlebars, wetsuits all can provide significant competitive advantages to those who have them—and equally significant hurdles for those who don't."

Kidder, then chairman of the Triathlon Federation's safety and rules committee, argued for "a definition of the bicycle which will ensure a

© Photo Run/Victor Sailer

Florence Griffith Joyner ran her World Championship preliminary heats in the "aerodynamic" suit, but stripped down for the finals.

relatively safe contest that will always be decided by the individual rather than by the equipment—a simple, affordable definition which will help this sport become what we want it to be: a true mass sport."

The staff of the sport's major magazine, *Triathlete*, disagreed. An unsigned editorial stated, "We believe that the choice of equipment becomes just another strategic racing consideration and should be left to the individual. The athlete who uncritically buys and uses the most expensive and 'sophisticated' equipment is just as vulnerable to defeat as the athlete who disregards those considerations."

Triathlete's editors added, "Maybe we should limit triathlons to one-speed beach cruisers. The sport would certainly be safe and more affordable. It just wouldn't be very exciting any more. Unnecessarily stringent rules will kill the very vitality that makes triathlons so attractive."

Technology would surely seduce runners too if its products aided our racing times more directly and dramatically. So far, we've generally avoided equipment gimmickry simply because it doesn't work very well.

I hope no new discovery changes that fact. It worried me, for instance, to see American sprinter Florence Griffith and the U.S. men's 400-meter relay team running their heats in speedskaters' suits at a World Championships competition in the late 1980s.

"It's supposed to be aerodynamic," said Griffith of her head-to-ankle suit, which might have cut down wind resistance and measurably increased speed. If it had, the copying would have been immediate and widespread.

Luckily the effect was underwhelming, as Griffith and the relay men all stripped down for their finals. Our sport won another round against expensive props.

Resist ads for products that promise to make you a better runner. Don't try to buy success.

Leg Products

My legs aren't much to look at. They're too short, thick, and scarred to show off. But I still hate to cover them up. I've never liked the month of

November, because my legs go into hiding then and stay there until spring.

This used to mean wrapping them in bulky cotton or crinkly nylon. Now, thanks to Jim Hill, I move more freely and quietly through the cold season.

Hill makes semi-tights. His pants are lighter than sweats and looser than tights. For me, they're the next-best choice after bare legs.

Hill's story is as remarkable as his product. His talent sprouted early in both running and business.

He competed in his first international race, the junior World Cross-Country, at 17. He ran the 5,000 at the first World Track Championships while still in college.

Hill then made a fast start in business. In his 20s, he was a young man with an old-fashioned sales approach—a throwback to simpler times when maverick inventors ruled the marketplace.

Today's best athletes make their names first, then sell them for use on clothing labels. They don't dirty their hands with manufacturing and sales details.

Jim Hill couldn't sell clothes on his reputation as a runner alone. But the name Hill did already loom large in innovative gear for runners.

Englishman Ron Hill, a leading marathoner of the early 1970s, wasn't happy with the shoes and clothes then on the market. He set about modifying them.

The reflective "spaceman" uniform this Hill wore in the 1972 Olympic Marathon was a short-lived oddity. But other designs survived the test of time. One was a pair of long pants.

The two Hills aren't related by blood, but are directly linked as tinkerers and businessmen. Jim felt uncomfortable in the running pants of that time.

"I didn't like cotton sweats," he said later. "I hated rainsuits. And I never cared for tights."

During a trip to Europe, Jim found a suitable combination of freedom, feel, and fit in Ron Hill pants. These weren't marketed in the U.S.

"I later wrote to his company and asked if I could act as a distributor in this country," said Jim. "I never heard back."

Rejection stirred him into action. Freshly graduated from the University of Oregon with a degree in finance ("I had learned how to use a calculator"), Jim decided in 1985 to make his own pants. SportHill was born with money raised from selling his car ("an expensive one that I didn't need").

For two years, he operated out of a small duplex in Eugene, Oregon. He was the company's only full-time worker.

While he started with the basic Ron Hill design, Jim's version feels and looks quite different. He uses a softer and stretchier cotton-polyester-Lycra material instead of nylon. The SportHill fit is somewhat more snug than its predecessor, while still not clinging like a second skin.

The result is a garment more modest than tights, warmer than a rainsuit, and less burdensome than sweats. It keeps a runner cozy in both cold and wet weather, yet allows unrestricted movement.

Meanwhile Jim Hill chose to move less freely than a young runner with his talent might. The growing business didn't allow him to be a nomadic professional athlete.

Take advantage of the technical advances that make running safer, more pleasant, and more exciting.

When asked about SportHill's interfering with his running, he responded, "I don't worry much about that. Very few runners will ever make enough money to be set for life. Not many even earn enough to live well *now*. I wanted to start a career that didn't depend on how I did in my latest race."

Eye Products

Who were those masked men? Five of the top seven finishers at the 1992 Men's Olympic Marathon Trial hid their eyes while running.

They wore sunglasses—those sleek, chic wraparound shades that are Darth Vaderizing running. Remember Vader, the "Star Wars" character who breathed heavily and shielded his eyes with black plastic?

You can't watch a race or open a magazine anymore without seeing half the celebrity runners masked. The Vaderizing has reached so far— to cloudy days and nighttime races, to awards platforms and interview circles—that it's time someone commented on it. I'd be glad to, thank you.

Maybe I'm an old fuddy-duddy. I resist leaping onto the leading edge of running fashion. Maybe I'm just old. I'd look silly dressing in styles designed for kids half my age. Or maybe I'm jealous. I can't wear this

> Keep running simple. Get along without most of the accessories that needlessly complicate the sport.

trendy item because shades wouldn't look so cool if worn over the thick bifocals that I'm blind without.

Whatever the reason, I think it's time for the Vaders of running to look at themselves in a mirror. Ask themselves, Is this a functional or a fashion item? Is it a better way to see or only a different way to *look*?

These shades do serve some practical purposes. Wearers could argue that squinting into the sun causes tension, which in turn leads to fatigue. They could say that wearing shades deflects wind, rain, and bugs from their eyes. They could even get really honest and say they're paid by the manufacturer to display this product.

Putting these sunglasses on high-visibility athletes is a promoter's dream. Shoe companies would kill for the exposure that shades-makers receive as viewers watch and cameras focus on the face, not the feet.

I'm not naive enough to think that Lasse Viren took off his Tigers and waved them around his head at the Montreal Olympics because his feet were burning. Skiers at the Winter Games don't hold their logoed skis up beside their heads to shake off the snow.

I wouldn't deny runners the right to make extra bucks by being moving advertising signs. I don't object to their thinking that a strip of colored plastic across their eyes makes them run more comfortably. I don't even mind their racing along with a fad.

What does bother me is what this fashion statement says about the wearers of shades. With the sunglasses, they seem to slip into a new personality.

The look—intended or not—is cool and distant at best, arrogant and menacing at worst. It seems to say, "Hey, I'm a star and I'm trying to hide behind this disguise. I don't want you to know who I really am, so leave me alone."

To all the Darth Vaders of running, I send this message: Run races in the sunglasses to fulfill whatever contractual obligations or personal needs you might have. Train in them even at night if you wish.

But please show us your faces in posed photos, in TV interviews, and on the victory stand. Flip the shades onto your forehead or twirl them in one hand if you must. Show us your eyes, the windows of the personality and emotions. Take off the mask. Show who you are and how you feel.

Reference Products

My dad, once a journalist himself, passed along an early lesson to me that I now give to my students as a sometimes-teacher of journalism: "You don't need to know everything. You only need to know where to *find* anything."

A great memory for everything you've read isn't a requirement of this job. But access to a great library is.

My personal library is pitifully small. Its three shelves occupy less than half of one wall in my writing room.

Most of the volumes there are my own: yearly diaries dating from 1959, raw book manuscripts, two binders of newsletters, and the finished books written and edited. A single filing cabinet drawer holds all my magazine articles with space left over for another 30 years of writing.

The only magazine that stays on a shelf for long is the one I contribute to, and the *Runner's World*s only go back a year. Other publications last no more than a month before they're recycled to another writer/fan in town.

Books, once read, usually get sent to the next reader. About the only ones I keep are the historical and statistical references needed regularly in writing.

I used to save every scrap of printed material that came through the door. But the accumulation mounted to the point where it threatened to push the family outside.

My library is skimpy. But my memory of what has been written and where to find copies stays fairly sharp despite a growing information overload, both personal and sportwise.

Three reference works sit in my permanent collection. They list all the books that aren't here anymore.

Ed Kozloff serves as librarian for the Detroit-area Motor City Striders. He sent me a computer printout listing hundreds of titles that he has collected and that club members can check out.

A Eugene friend, Norm Lumian, passed along a slim volume he'd once bought on a trip to Europe. It's titled *British Track and Field Literature, 1275 to 1968* (Athletics Arena, 1969). The entries begin with a 13th-century running poem called "Havelok the Dane." The oldest book, *Manly Exercises*, dates from 1864.

RW editors Marty Post and Bob Wischnia collaborated on the best single sourcebook. *Running: A Guide to the Literature* (Garland) carries their minireviews on most of the books in print at the time of the guide's publication.

Finding the names of these books isn't hard. Finding the books themselves is. Many originated with small publishers that have gone out of business. Most books didn't sell well enough to stay in print for long.

You might find them in libraries, public and private. Or you could search the used-book stores. Two specialty houses—Cedarwinds and Books for Runners—are now in the business of preserving and distributing these treasures.

Reading the Cedarwinds and Books for Runners offerings, and scanning the history books on running publishing, recalls the magic moments when authors first handed their messages to me. These lists remind me of old favorites.

Start your own running library. Adopt book authors as the best coaches and role models you'll ever know.

This isn't necessarily the greatest literature in terms of writing style. Other books may have enjoyed better reviews and sales. The mark of greatness for my favorites was that their writers said exactly the right things at just the right time.

Few of these works remain on my shelves. They're out of sight but not mind.

You can give away or throw away a great book. But you never lose one.

20

Better

Diets

George Sheehan III, the good doctor's son and business manager, is a clever writer in his own right. Commenting on the concoctions that Chinese women runners supposedly ingest, he noted, "It looks as though the pasta dinner will become passé. Worm-and-turtle stew will be the rage. 'Just Eat It' will be the cry."

Chinese coach Ma Junren claimed that the fungus that grows on caterpillars and the soup made from soft-shelled turtles fueled his record-setting athletes. "This is all natural," Ma said in answer to charges that his runners were drugged. "Chinese people have been drinking it for hundreds of years."

These elixirs are available worldwide. But before you rush to your nearest Chinatown, arm yourself with a few facts.

First, these products aren't cheap. A packet of 20 worms sells for $35 in New York City's Chinatown and might be worthless by itself.

William C. Rhoden wrote in the *New York Times*, "The [Ma] potion's power comes not exclusively from the worm or the fungus but from both being used in combination with other herbs . . . Ma said he had discovered the perfect mixture."

He wouldn't reveal the formula but planned to market it eventually. News of his alleged discovery gave him exactly what he wanted—a smoke screen and a tantalizing free-advertising campaign.

Talk of exotic food supplements diverted attention from what might really lie behind China's sudden success in distance running. It reminded us of Lasse Viren deflecting rumors of blood-doping 20 years earlier by saying that his secret was drinking "reindeer milk."

Advance advertising for Ma's product fed the illusions of readers who think they can take magic by mouth. People who wouldn't dream of taking drugs might spend a day's pay on a vile-tasting foodstuff that promises them faster times.

It's a seductive idea. It capitalizes on the widespread suspicion that a mystery ingredient is missing from our diet. We think that by finding it we'll suddenly perform better.

Call it the "bee-pollen pitch," so named for a potion that enjoyed brief popularity in the 1980s. It all but vanished from the running marketplace when we learned that it didn't work as well as promised.

Try worm-and-turtle stew if you wish. Prepare to be disappointed.

No legal dietary supplement has ever worked as dramatically as Coach Ma claims, and none ever will. Nutrition doesn't work that way.

At best, diet's effects on runners are indirect. Eat right and you can train right. The training, not the food, is what makes you a better runner. No one ever just ate his or her way to great running.

Deficiencies do sometimes occur. Runners can suffer from carbohydrate starvation or chronic dehydration, for instance.

But dietary problems far more often arise from excesses than from missing ingredients. We suffer from eating too much meat and fat, too much sugar and salt, too many chemicals and colorings, or simply too much of everything. We might eat what our body chemistry can't tolerate. We might eat too close to runs and races.

You can correct deficiencies without paying a costly visit to Chinatown. Any neighborhood store carries all the ingredients you could need.

You can correct excesses by observing the simple rules: When in doubt about an item, don't eat it. Before running, err on the side of eating too little rather than too much, and too soon rather than too late.

Intolerable Diets

Orville Atkins was in bad shape the last time I'd seen him. That had been about three years before.

Running had been a big part of his life. He'd migrated from Ontario to California in the early 1960s to train with coach Mihaly Igloi's high-powered group.

Atkins had placed as high as fifth in the Boston Marathon. He'd attended most of the Olympics, as a viewer, since 1964.

When last we'd met, Orville couldn't run anymore. He wasn't injured or tired of running. A mysterious ailment had stolen his health.

"If I run one day, I'm sick for the next week," he'd said then. "The doctors have given me all sorts of tests and ruled out the worst possibilities."

They couldn't find anything worse than allergies. Atkins was allergic to pollen, dust, feathers, and other airborne culprits.

Treating these conditions didn't help. Stopping running (which he did for eight months) didn't make the problem go away either. It only kept it from getting worse.

The awful truth was that running, which he had done so long and so well, made him sick. Could someone be allergic to it?

Doctors lost patience with this patient. They hinted that the trouble was all in his head. But Atkins knew his body well enough to feel that something was amiss physically.

He looked for his own answers ("I became convinced that I had chronic fatigue syndrome"), and for a doctor who'd tell him exactly what was wrong and what to do about it. He finally found one.

As Orville again began reciting his tiresome history, this doctor stopped him in the first two minutes. He said, "I think you might have some food allergies."

George Sheehan would have liked this doctor. Sheehan had long said that physicians give too little thought to diet in general and dietary sensitivities in particular.

Food allergies usually go undiagnosed, said Sheehan, because there is no easy test for them and they aren't life-threatening. He said with any recurring problem of the skin, breathing, or gut to suspect foods as the cause.

I know I'm allergic to chocolate. It gives me headaches, itches, and the skin of a teenager.

Sensitivities seem to grow with age. The chocolate reactions began in my late 30s.

My breathing went bonkers in my mid-40s. An allergist diagnosed exercise-induced asthma, prescribing a drug but also saying, "You might be sensitive to dairy products." I quit using them and the problem (as well as need for the drug) went away.

The treatment for food allergies isn't to take medicine but to take items out of the diet. Sheehan listed milk and wheat as the most common offenders.

Orville Atkins eliminated those and other items. He said when we met again, "I also cut out nuts—I used to eat lots of peanut butter. I cut way down on caffeine and sugar—I was a Coke guzzler. I even quit drinking beer because of the hops.

"I could hardly believe the results. The change after 10 days of omitting all foods I was allergic to, and actually eating very few types of foods, was like being born again."

But he added, "If I eat even one pat of butter with dinner now, I'll wake up that night in a cold sweat."

As long as Orville watches his diet, he can run. "I only run every other day now at about eight-and-a-half-minute or slower pace," he said.

But getting back at all has put a happy ending on his story.

Low-Fat Diets

I'd been slow to answer the call of nutrition's true believers. I'd resisted their arguments as either distasteful or irrelevant.

The food-as-poison argument hadn't swayed me. I couldn't imagine that everything these experts said is bad for us really is when eating it gives so much pleasure.

The food-as-medicine argument hadn't won me over either. I wasn't about to eat what was good for me if it tasted terrible.

The food-as-fuel argument had failed too. Thinking of food only as "super unleaded" going in the tank to make me run farther and faster would have spoiled the fun of eating.

The food-as-fat argument made sense generally but hadn't been a personal concern. Run enough and you can eat your fill without getting too heavy, I'd always thought.

I was running a little less than I once did, and weighing a little more. But I tolerated a few extra pounds when the option was deprivation. Dieting was intolerable.

Tom Miller agreed. He's my height but more blocky of build. He's also more of a runner (a veteran of 100-plus marathons) and more of an authority on how the body works (a Ph.D. candidate in exercise science).

Miller told me at his running camp in Utah, "I've lost 15 to 20 pounds in the past few months without dieting. I'm eating more than ever." Now there was a winning argument!

He credited his then-wife, Kathy Melby, for this transformation. She runs with the group he coaches, and is a college-trained nutritionist who owns health-food stores in Salt Lake City and Las Vegas.

Like many of us old-line runners, Miller had never given his diet much thought. "Kathy changed that," he said. "She convinced me to watch my fat consumption. In fact, that's really all I watch."

Like most Americans, including many runners, Tom ate too much fatty food. "Americans typically eat 40 to 50 percent of their calories as fat," said Melby at the camp. This causes all sorts of health consequences, the most obvious being obesity.

Melby added, "I recommend cutting fat to no more than 20 percent. That's half of 'normal,' and this change alone will have profound effects on your health and weight."

She noted, "You need some fat. I've tried to cut it down as low as Nathan Pritikin recommended—to 10 percent—but I was hungry all the time, never satisfied."

Bear with me through some math. It leads to a simple conclusion.

Twenty percent of an average 2,000-calorie day of eating equals 400 calories of fat, but food labels express fat content in grams. A gram of fat carries nine calories, so the day's limit would be 45 grams.

Tom Miller said he doesn't exceed 35 grams. He could blow that quota on one Big Mac or a bowl of Haagen Dazs ice cream, leaving no room for anything fatty the rest of the day. Or he could spend that amount little by little throughout the day on lower-fat foods—the choice he prefers.

Eat a high-carbo, low-fat diet all the time—not just before races. Eat for health and pleasure, not just performance.

This diet doesn't require serious deprivation. It doesn't mean buying foods with names you can't pronounce or shopping only in happy hippie marketplaces.

This is simply a matter of rebalancing what you already eat and can buy in any store. "Make meat or cheese a side dish instead of the centerpiece of the meal as it is for most Americans," said Kathy Melby. "Build your meals around complex carbohydrates [pasta and potatoes, for example], and eat your fill of them. It's impossible to get too many."

Read labels and count fat grams until you know the totals by heart. Learn how many grams you are comfortable with.

Excess fat eaten equals more fat stored. Eat less of it, wear less of it.

Liquid Diets

As Willie Mtolo fumbled at his right wrist in the 22nd mile of the New York City Marathon, he set ABC's commentary team to guessing. "What's he trying to do?" asked Jim McKay.

"He may be looking for his split times?" said Marty Liquori. "Whatever it is, he's wasting motion," said Joan Samuelson.

Something small and white dropped from Mtolo's hand to the road. He was later seen popping one of those objects into his mouth before moving toward his victory.

Asked afterward what was in his armband, Mtolo laughed it off as "just a magic thing." The next morning's *New York Times* reported that he'd wrapped five glucose pills in a Velcro band.

These pills that he gobbled for energy and then diluted with water weren't the reason the South African won in New York. They weren't magical but surely were unusual.

Taking sugar in concentrated doses during marathons has fallen out of favor since Frank Shorter made defizzed Coke his drink of choice on the way to his 1972 Olympic gold medal. Sugared drinks later scored low marks in lab tests.

The folks in white coats concluded that sugar slowed the absorption of water, which is what a runner really needs. They said sweet liquids stayed in the stomach, sloshing uselessly.

Science came out on the side of plain water or very weak sugar solutions. From this laboratory evidence grew the special athletic drinks served during races.

On-the-road evidence tells a different story. The slower the runners travel and the longer they take to finish, the more they need some calories as they run. For them, sugar does seem to go where it can work against exhaustion, and caffeine seems to speed it there.

Drink early and often during long runs and races. Consider adding sugar and caffeine to the liquid diet.

Tom Osler made a believer of me. His formula for dramatically extending distances came in two parts.

The sport has gradually adopted the first part, taking the walking breaks that were the subject of an earlier chapter, and forgotten the second—taking sweetened, caffeinated drinks. Osler preferred heavily sugared tea.

I might not have believed the first trick if the walks hadn't carried me two and a half times farther than my longest nonstop distance. I might not have swallowed his drinking trick if not for an incident at the Boston Marathon.

This happened just after Osler's *Serious Runner's Handbook* came out, and I still ran mainly on water. I hoped to break three hours that day, and my 25-mile time put me within reach of that goal if the pace held up.

© Photo Run/Victor Sailer

Take advantage of water breaks early and often during long runs or races.

It didn't. The last 1.2 miles took almost 12 minutes to complete.

Someone handed me a can of Coke at the finish line, and I downed it in two gulps. A few minutes later, my paralysis had miraculously lifted and I ran back to my hotel a mile away. If only that could have been the 26th mile instead of the 27th!

In all my marathons since then, I've taken sweet drinks when they could do some good. They've never failed me.

At best, the sugar, caffeine, and water gave a quick surge of energy which wasn't (as doubters have suggested) followed by a plunge. At worst, the effect was neutral and these treats tasted good.

Any of the full-strength, naturally sweetened and caffeinated drinks will do—Coke, Pepsi, Dr. Pepper, Mountain Dew. But my favorite is Snapple juice-flavored iced tea, with all the sweetness of sodas but none of the chemicals or bubbles.

When to drink? Early and often—at least at the starting line, the half-way point, and around 20 miles if the race is a marathon.

You can't expect the aid stations to supply soft drinks, you won't want to seek out vending machines, and you can't strap a can on your arm as Willie Mtolo did with his glucose pills. So enlist your own drink-server or seed the course in advance with these legal, nonprescription miracle drugs.

Solid Diets

This was a first. And when you're as deeply into a running lifetime as I am, firsts come sparingly.

This was my first New York City Marathon. But other than the surroundings, I expected it to go like any other marathon.

For sure I'd planned no changes in eating practices. I came from the Arthur Lydiard school of diet.

"I've never seen anyone collapse of malnutrition in a race," the New Zealand coach once said. "But I've seen plenty of runners fall out of races for the opposite reason—from eating too much of the wrong foods, too late."

Run on the fuel you stocked up on a day or two before the race, said Lydiard and others. Eat sparingly or not at all that morning.

Eat *during* a race? Are you kidding?

I didn't completely buy the scientific party line that anything much stronger than water is wasted during a race. Certain tests have shown that the hard-working body doesn't digest the additives.

This might be true for bodies traveling at five minutes per mile. Those running much slower might react differently.

Mine does. Heavily sugared drinks have always given me mid-race boosts. But I'd never dared take solids along the way, and didn't plan to start at New York.

Experiment with eating immediately before and during marathon-type runs. Start by munching on sports bars.

The two Powerbars in my bag were to serve other purposes. One was to be "breakfast" during the long wait for the later-than-normal start. The other was to ride in my waistband to become a late "lunch" after the race.

Powerbars might not be the best possible meals. But they're more portable than pancakes or pasta.

My first bar went down several hours before the start. This might have been too late to do much good, but it seemed early enough not to do any harm.

The second Powerbar never reached the finish. Hunger overwhelmed restraint in mid-race.

I fantasized about stopping and begging a meal at one of the dozens of course-side cafés. Their aromas grew more tantalizing with each mile.

Instead of stopping, I tore into the Powerbar on the Queensboro Bridge and nibbled half the apple-cinnamon glob between 15 and 17 miles. The other half broke off and fell to the road, probably to gum up some runner's shoe.

Eating this way could have been a dumb move to make at the worst possible time. It violated a cardinal rule of racing, which is to test no new trick on raceday.

The last 10 miles of a marathon are hard enough to run without adding a bellyache. But mine never ached.

I don't want this to sound like an unpaid testimonial and can't prove that the Powerbar earns any credit. But something gave me an unusual lift that lasted all 10 miles. For one of the rare times, the splits for the halves were negative.

This story won't be news to Jeff Galloway. After the race, I read of his early experience with Powerbars.

Test all pre-race and mid-race drinks and foods in training. Try new items and timing before raceday.

He also told of first learning their benefits at New York City. He too started eating shortly after the halfway point, and reported feeling better and recovering more quickly than with his old fasting routine.

Galloway's first try wouldn't be his last. Nor would mine.

21

Better

Cures

The newspaper reporter on the phone unwittingly struck a nerve of mine. His assignment was to look into the myth that won't die: the charge that running is hazardous to our orthopedic health.

Doug Thomas of the *Omaha World-Herald* already had his yes-it's-risky quotations and facts. Now he wanted someone to defend the sport.

"Would you comment?" he asked. Oh, would I!

Unlike many writers who tackle this topic, Thomas isn't antirunning. He researched all sides and wrote a balanced story—meaning readers could read whatever they wanted into it.

Nonrunners could find more reasons never to run. Runners could find reasons for hope.

Injury statistics alarm runners who don't know the whole story—and amuse the sport's critics, who don't care to know it all. Dr. Joe Ellis, a podiatrist who treats running injuries by the hundreds, said that 75 to 80 percent of runners who put in more than 25 miles a week can expect to be injured.

The apparent message here: the less you run, the healthier you'll be. Taking that advice to its logical end, the way to stay perfectly safe is to run nothing.

Dr. Roger Christensen, of the Cooper Clinic in Dallas, used to run. He switched to other activities with lesser orthopedic demands after completing several marathons in the mid-1980s.

Dr. Christensen told Thomas, "I think runners can avoid injuries. But I think anybody who's running four or five times a week and continues that over a long period of time is going to have long-term damage."

He did make an exception for certain top athletes who train two or three times this often. They also run up to 10 times the safe mileage that his boss, Dr. Kenneth Cooper, prescribes for fitness runners.

"Probably the biggest difference between a world- and national-class marathon runner and somebody like you or me is that they are orthopedically gifted," said Christensen. "They're people who for whatever reason can handle 70 or 80 miles a week of running without breaking down."

There's some truth in all of this. I admitted to the reporter from Omaha, "Sure, running causes some problems. Total safety is too much to expect from this or any sport."

Realize that you run a 50-50 chance of getting hurt in any year, and that most running injuries are self-inflicted.

Runners get hurt, but seldom seriously or permanently. Few of the injuries even rate a doctor's visit, or require any treatment more sophisticated than rest and aspirin.

Few injuries do any more than disrupt the running routine, which probably needed changing anyway or we wouldn't have gotten hurt. Few of them disrupt life outside the run.

Few injuries fail to heal in a few days to a few weeks. Few become chronic unless we chronically make the same mistakes.

Maybe we need a milder word here than "injury" for what happens to us. We're not talking here about the results of a violent collision between a pass receiver and a defensive end, but only about repeated minicollisions of our own body weight with the earth.

Football players talk about major trauma, big medical bills, and possibly permanent damage. Runners talk about problems that rank in severity with headaches and toothaches.

This doesn't make our problems any less real. A sore point the size of a dime—located at the wrong spot on a bone, muscle, or tendon—can stop a runner.

But our pain comes more from the head than from the body. The loss of running hurts worse than the injury. Refusing to accept that loss, failing to wait out the pain, rushing the recovery timetable, neglecting to correct the causes—all prolong and intensify the pain.

Sure, running can be risky. But the runner controls the degree of risk and can usually keep it acceptable.

Medical Cures

The question before the house was why doctors weren't living up to their promises of making runners more healthy.

This night's welcome-to-Eugene party for Australian national coach Tony Benson had become an impromptu clinic. The room held three coaches besides Benson who'd taken runners to world competition, plus a world-class orthopedic surgeon and a major track meet director.

The Australian coach aimed his question at the doctor, Stan James. "Why, with the best sports medicine ever, are we seeing more injuries than ever? We pour so much money into the program to keep the kids healthy, but it's not preventing injury."

> Realize that few injuries are serious, and that most respond quickly to self-treatment.

Dr. James let other guests stab at answers first. They fingered the usual suspects: shoes, surfaces, training methods, overracing.

Benson said that better detection and definition of problems is itself a problem. This creates more injuries, real or imagined.

"We never heard of iliotibial band syndrome or chondromalacia," he said of his days as an international athlete 20 years earlier. "The only self-diagnosis I allow my kids to make now is, 'I have a sore leg.' "

Someone mentioned that more runners get hurt because there are more to be hurt now than in the 1970s. Improved shoes and sports-medicine advances have propped up biomechanical misfits who would have dropped out early back then. They can stay more active but must see doctors more often.

Sports doctors may have failed us, said Benson, by raising false hopes. "Maybe runners go closer to the line [between maximum training and injury], instead of backing off at the first sign of a problem, because they think the support system is better."

It's much better. But it can never be good enough so long as we believe that doctors hold the final answer to an injury.

Everyone has a breaking point. Look long and hard enough for it, and you're guaranteed to find it.

Doctors can push that point higher than it otherwise would be. They can prescribe painkillers, orthotics, and cross-training. They can perform surgery. But without the patient's help, they can't stop the injury from recurring.

We runners must take ultimate responsibility for getting well and staying well. Doctors don't fail us nearly as often as we fail ourselves.

Dr. James recalled studying hundreds of his injured-runner cases 15 years before. "Nothing has changed since then," he said. "Runners still get hurt at the same rates and for the same reasons now. In more than two-thirds of cases, the cause is a training error."

He pointed to the familiar trio of mistakes: too far, too fast, too often. "Most people train by reaching out in the dark for a hot stove," he said. They know they've done too much only when they shout, 'There, I found it!' and get burned by an injury."

The trick to staying healthy, said James, is recognizing the difference between maximum and *optimum* training. Maximum is seeing how much work is required to break you. Optimum is seeing how little work you need while getting the results you want.

Dr. James's prescription for optimal training: "First, convince yourself that you can optimize fitness or competitive capabilities at a point far below the level where there is a danger of injury. Second, be willing to settle for what may sound like a small amount of training."

He favored a hard-easy approach and thinks that "three good-quality workouts a week is all most people really need to optimize results and minimize risks. My definition of an easy day is not doing anything that might foul up the hard day—which should be a delightful, challenging, satisfying workout when you feel fresh going into it."

James said the hard-easy system makes sense both athletically and medically. Optimizing our training load lightens the doctor's caseload.

Run through minor soreness that eases during warm-up. Stop for any pain that grows worse as you go along.

Cold Cures

Dr. George Sheehan always treated the common cold with utmost respect, but little else. He once explained his hands-off approach in a talk to runners.

"If you do everything right—take aspirin, extra vitamins, cough syrup, decongestant, and chicken soup—you'll get over the cold in seven days," said Dr. Sheehan. "If you do nothing at all and just wait out the symptoms, you'll get well in a week."

I prefer the one-week recovery plan over the seven-day system. The simplest and cheapest thing to take for a cold is nothing.

The problem for a runner comes from misreading that word "nothing." It doesn't mean ignoring the symptoms and changing nothing in your running routine.

Nothing means exactly that: doing no running during at least the worst days of the cold's stay.

Sheehan said, "I treat a cold with respect. It represents a breakdown in the defense system. It is an early warning of exhaustion."

A cold is nature's way of telling you to back off. You don't so much catch one as it catches *you* when your defenses have eroded.

Overworking leaves you vulnerable to this ever-present virus that you normally might fight off. Continued hard work in the face of symptoms can turn a mild weeklong cold into a nasty set of complications lasting far longer.

Don't think, as I once did, that because you cough up and blow out gunk by running through a cold that you're clearing it away sooner. Stirring up your already irritated respiratory system this way may complicate an otherwise simple illness.

Amby Burfoot thought he'd just caught a little cold. The *Runner's World* editor and onetime Boston Marathon winner said later, "It seemed like a superficial thing, and I didn't think it would affect me."

He raced a 10K as he was coming down with the cold. It later deteriorated into pneumonia that hospitalized Amby for 10 days and kept him from running normally for three months.

I met my usual quota of two colds one year, first in the winter and then in the summer. Their treatments were as different as their outcomes.

February's cold came with a mild case of the flu. I couldn't run in that condition so I took most of a week off. The cold vanished without a trace in that week.

With July's cold, I took just one day off at its start. The sore throat and nagging cough didn't go away on schedule, but hung on far beyond the standard week.

George Sheehan has said, "If a cold lasts more than a week to 10 days, you can assume it isn't a simple cold any more. You probably have developed a secondary infection."

The most common complications are chronic sinus, throat, and bronchial infections. I developed all three last summer, and they lasted for months while also helping to trigger exercise-induced asthma.

This episode raised a healthy fear in me of long-lasting colds. I vowed then to treat any cold with nothing but the greatest respect. Skipping runs for a few days now to avoid weeks or months of misery later sounded like a wise investment.

Rest during all illnesses (including colds), which are your body's signals that you've already run too much and need time off.

The chance to test this wisdom came with the next winter's cold. I did nothing for it—didn't gobble aspirin, didn't megadose on vitamin C, didn't take Nyquil or Sudafed. I'm most proud of running nothing for much of this cold's duration. The hardest thing for a runner to do is nothing—giving up the fight and letting nature take its course on its own timetable.

I could have run, wanted to run, but didn't run for the seven days of this cold. By then, it had almost run its normal one-week course unimpeded.

Rest Cures

The immediate facts themselves told an amazing story: American Bob Kennedy ran 5,000 meters in 13:05 and then 13:02.

These were the fastest ever by a runner born in this country. Only South African native Sydney Maree stood higher on the all-time U.S. list.

Kennedy's times spoke for themselves but didn't tell the full story. For that, you had to look back a few months to a time when he couldn't run at all.

Kennedy had announced the previous fall that he had to add mileage if he was to keep pace with the Africans. That winter, he joined Todd

© Photo Run/Victor Sailer

Bob Kennedy is proof positive that giving injuries the rest they need when they need it can pay off.

Williams, a notoriously hard worker, for some training and soon came down with a stress fracture. (The same ailment later claimed Williams.)

This wasn't a bad break for Kennedy. He might even look at it now as a lucky one. Without it, he might have run a full menu of winter and spring races before going on the European summer circuit.

Few Americans ever hold their form that long. On the other hand, U.S. running history is rich with stories of athletes coming off injuries to do their best.

They trained themselves to a peak and went over the edge. Nature then gave them the needed time off from running that they wouldn't have taken voluntarily. They came back fresh, hungry, and relieved— and nowadays strong from their alternate training—to achieve success that might not have been possible without the break.

Bill Rodgers wrote in *Masters Running and Racing*, "One of my greatest moments and one of my most disappointing moments came within a few months of each other in 1976." He could have added that another proud moment came shortly after the disappointment.

Rodgers ran "one of the most intense races of my life" to make the Olympic team that year. Then he injured himself while training for Montreal, where he placed only 40th. Coming off that injury, he won the first of his four New York City Marathons.

You know that Alberto Salazar debuted at New York in 1980 with 2:09:41. You might not recall that injuries often limited his training to the swimming pool during the months leading up to that race.

Joan Samuelson has said, "I might not have won the Olympic Marathon if I hadn't injured myself that spring." The famous knee that allowed her to run the 1984 trial just 17 days after arthroscopic surgery had limited her training during the two months prior to the race.

"I was in too-good shape in March of that year," Samuelson said. "The injury allowed me to peak at just the right time, for Los Angeles instead of Olympia."

Mary Slaney knows more than any American about these recurring cycles of up, followed by down, leading to another up. She seldom gets more than a few months between injuries but keeps rebounding strongly.

Bob Kennedy stands as further proof of how high a runner can bounce back within a few months after falling down. His spring break prepared him for a better summer. As surely as one season follows another, a high cycle follows a low.

22

Better

Coaches

Think for a moment about who had the most to do with starting you running. Who first set you on the path that you still follow?

My list starts in the family—with a dad, uncles, and a brother who were all track athletes and fans. They showed me the path but never said I had to take it.

Another man guided me in my first halting steps along a path that now reaches back into the 1950s. Until now, I've never given him full credit for his help because it was so subtle.

I hadn't thought about Dean Roe in too long when an item in *USA Today* several years ago reminded me of him. It listed him as a nominee for national coach of the year.

A later report in an Iowa newspaper filled in the details. He didn't win the national title, but was honored as his region's top coach in girls' basketball.

Mr. Roe (that was how we always addressed him, never as "Coach" or "Dean"; meeting him much later, I would still call him "Mister") now coached only the one sport. But he was once the coach for all seasons in our little town.

In the article, he claimed me as one of his nine state track champions. The least I can do is recognize him at last as my first coach.

I've written before of not being coached in high school. That's technically true, since I wrote my own training plan almost from the start. But it's unfair to Mr. Roe to leave this story unfinished. His influence was more profound and lasting than writing workouts.

His coaching career began at Coin High School. To say that his first football team went undefeated that fall is as inadequate as saying that the Sioux won at Little Big Horn. Mr. Roe's team averaged 69 points a game to its opponents' 3 and was named state champion.

© Rich Etchberger

Find a coach or advisor who'll judge your running and plot your improvements more objectively than you could.

That fall, he became a deity in this country town. A whole generation of boys and girls grew up trying to please him so that he would make winners of us.

His magic didn't work on me in football or basketball. He had too little raw material to work with there.

Track was the last hope, and a slim one at that. Mr. Roe treated this sport more lightly than the serious team games.

His approach to track was: If you want to train, I'll time you, and if you want to travel to meets, I'll take you. If not, I won't force you. I wanted to run and race, and he provided the setting.

Find a coach or adviser who'll judge your running and plot your improvements more objectively than you could.

This coach believed in team effort and not the glorification of individuals. He didn't fully understand distance runners. He didn't know why I ran alone, without being told or watched.

But Mr. Roe knew enough to leave the running to me. I didn't need his discipline after becoming more demanding of myself than he was with any athlete.

What I needed was the confidence of knowing that someone I believed in also believed in me. Mr. Roe knew what to say, when.

At our last state meet together, he said, "I'm as proud of you as any athlete I've ever coached, including those who won the state championship in football and played in the state basketball tournament. Because you've done the most with the least talent."

Coming from him, that was the supreme compliment. All these years later, each new run or race is a tribute to his early inspiration and support.

I wasn't the only one to receive these gifts. Norm Johnston carried them to a national championship in the high hurdles and within three places of the 1968 Olympic decathlon team. Rex Harvey still competes as a masters decathlete.

The truest measure of a coach's success isn't what athletes do while they're with him, but what they take with them when they leave his team. By this standard, Dean Roe sent hundreds of winners into the world.

Coach Bowerman

Writers oversimplify people by reducing them to a clause. They limit Kenny Moore by calling him only "a writer for *Sports Illustrated*" and Bill Bowerman by labeling him simply as "the father of Nike."

There's much more to both of them. And their stories are bound up in a single package.

The label doesn't say that, long before Nike, Bowerman was an innovative coach at the University of Oregon. We also might forget that, long before *SI*, Moore made two Olympic teams by using Bowerman's principles.

"He thought it was immoral to burn somebody out at 22," Moore told reporter Curtis Anderson. "He used college running as a foundation for better running later in life and a more expressive life. He was very proud of that."

The coach was proud that Moore only narrowly missed an Olympic medal at age 28, and even prouder of what he has done since. Moore was enormously grateful to his mentor, and would pay Bowerman back with the book (as yet, unpublished) that only Kenny could write.

He previewed the book-in-progress in an article for his university's alumni magazine. In the article Moore told of an early clash with Bowerman over training approaches.

"I persisted in trying to slog the 100 miles per week that his good friend, Arthur Lydiard, recommended to his runners," wrote Moore. Runners thought that was the magic formula in the 1960s.

Bowerman demanded to know, "Are you in this to do mindless labor, or do you want to improve?" When the young runner voted for improvement, the coach told him, "You can't improve if you're sick or injured all the time."

Moore continued to log high mileage. "Work for its own dumb sake is a hard habit to break, tied up as it is with ambition," he wrote later.

"By the spring of my sophomore year, fed up with my being sick and injured all the time, Bowerman closed his hands around my neck, lifted me off the ground, and told me that he wanted my oath that from now on I would take two or three recovery days of jogging and stretching between each remotely taxing workout. As I was blacking out, I submitted."

Rather than risk his neck, Moore trained Bowerman's way for three weeks. His best two-mile time had been 9:30. He suddenly dropped to 8:48 while beating the defending national champion, Dale Story of Oregon State.

Moore recalled, "It finally began to penetrate my thick skull that I had to rise above the world's fixation with sheer work. I had to attend to my own eccentric physiology.

"I accepted easy days into my life. I stopped counting miles. Over the next eight years, the one long run that Bowerman permitted me every 10 days would transform me into a runner capable of finishing fourth in the 1972 Olympic Marathon."

Moore added that "since then—tossing around in a world largely inhabited by people who have never learned how to compete and not let it take over their personality, who've never learned how to peak when it counts, or take a joke, or stand up to a tyrant, or have faith in their own thinking even if it is kind of strange—I have come to exult in having been pounded into shape by Bowerman's ceaseless, consternating imagination."

> Read the books by running's great advisers, and attend their lectures. Ask them questions about your running.

Bill Bowerman gave Kenny Moore the courage to walk away from Stanford Law School and become a writer. Later Moore would write the biography of the man who held him up by the figurative neck and asked in so many words, "Are you in this life to do mindless labor, or do you want to do your best work?"

The best of the best would go into the Bowerman book.

Coach Manley

We were nothing but two boys looking for adventure the day we met at a summer track meet in Chicago. We'd come to run a race unknown in high school and seldom contested anywhere else at the time, a 3,000-meter steeplechase.

He was down from Milwaukee and would enter the University of Wisconsin in the fall. I was in from Iowa and would soon begin writing about running as a high school senior. It was my second steeple and his first.

I just nipped him that day, 10:01 to 10:02, and must have known when to quit. I never tried this event again.

The other boy was the only great-runner-to-be I ever beat. He has been a constant force in U.S. distance running for more than 30 years.

Mike Manley became a Pan-American Games steeplechase winner and an Olympian in 1972. Shortly after turning 40 in 1982, he became the first American master to break 30 minutes in the 10K and 2:20 in the marathon. I'm a longtime admirer of all that he has done and continues to do.

We accidentally wound up in the same town of Eugene. Mike had first come here for coaching by the master, Bill Bowerman. He was one of four Bowerman distance runners to make the 1972 Olympic team.

Manley himself took up coaching—at the high school and junior college levels, and now as a freelancer. He carries on many of Bowerman's practices, including teaming runners up to increase the chances of an individual's succeeding.

Kenny Moore noted in a *Sports Illustrated* article that success in running often occurs in "clusters." He wrote of the sprinters now gathered around coach John Smith in Los Angeles and around coach Tom Tellez in Houston.

Moore could have mentioned his own work along with Manley in the Bowerman cluster of 20 to 25 years earlier. Or the Florida Track Club cluster in the Frank Shorter–Jack Bacheler years. Or the Greater Boston cluster that produced Bill Rodgers and the young Alberto Salazar.

Moore might have said, as Shorter has, that one problem with Americans these days is their go-it-alone tendencies. They need more teamwork in training to draw the best from one another.

The best current proof of this theory's merit comes from Mike Manley's team in Eugene. This group doesn't even have a name.

But no set of training partners had more say in the makeup of the 1993 World Championships team. Manley coached five U.S. runners who qualified in four different events.

The greatest compliment to Manley was Ken Martin's asking for his coaching. Martin was almost 35 years old and had been a coach himself. He knew enough to manage his own training.

Yet Martin moved back to Eugene (where he'd run in college), came to Manley, and asked for his help and the support of his team. Runners who want to be the best seek out the best.

Coach Salazar

He appeared as a mystery runner at the Spring Classic, a Portland 8K where I helped with the radio coverage. He didn't wear a low number, because he'd entered late, and his name didn't make the invited-runner list.

The reporter on the course could only say early that "number 75 is running away with the race." We finally learned it was Jim Farmer.

Farmer had moved to Oregon from North Carolina for the same reason that other runners had come here from Minnesota, Arizona, Montana, and California. They'd hoped the magic that made Alberto Salazar the runner he was a dozen years ago would rub off on them.

Nike supports Team Salazar, which Alberto began coaching soon after announcing his own semiretirement in 1992. He could still race well, as shown by his victory two years later in South Africa's Comrades ultramarathon. But his own running now ranked a distant second to his coaching.

Time added to the Salazar legend that drew young runners to him. His best marathon time stood for 12 years as America's fastest.

He won the New York City Marathon three straight times. No one else from here has even won it once since then.

He ran 2:08s and 2:09s five times. The total of sub-2:10 marathons for all Americans in the next 10 years would be just two.

Time also had given Salazar perspective on his own career. He could see why it was so good, and why so short.

Alberto worked incredibly hard. This served him well at first and hurt him later.

He made his first Olympic team at 21 and won his first New York Marathon at 22. But chronic injuries and illnesses had eaten away his prodigious skills before his 25th birthday.

He kept trying, kept hoping that his strong will would whip his unwilling body back into its earlier shape. He took 10 years to realize it would never happen.

"It was definitely hard and frustrating for many years," he told writer Philip Levinson. "Now I'm able to look back and be thankful for the races and short career that I had.

"I look at it positively. I can use my hard-earned knowledge to try to keep others from making the same mistakes I did."

His main mistake was not fully repaying his fatigue debts. He didn't recover well enough after his hard workouts and races.

Salazar regretted none of the work he had done. He only wished that he had rested more between the big efforts.

"How you train the month after a marathon is as important as how you train the month prior to the race," he wrote in *Runner's World*. "Take this from someone who shortened his career considerably—not because I overtrained but because I never rested properly after a marathon."

He now recommended taking a full month to return to normal mileage—running 25 percent of normal the first week, 50 percent the next two weeks, then 75 percent for a final week. Of course, this hadn't been his own practice.

"I felt I was indestructible," he said in the Levinson interview. "I thought I could train as hard as I wanted year-round.

"That really burned me out in the long run. The human body isn't meant to take this kind of stress continuously, year after year."

Alberto Salazar now had a second chance at age 35. He could train Jim Farmer and teammates hard, rest them well, and hope to see them racing longer, if not better, than their coach had.

Coach Connelly

Running needs more Pat Connellys—or Connollys, if you prefer. Two of them live in the Los Angeles area, and both were high-achieving athletes who turned to coaching.

One is a woman who spells her last name with an *o*. This Pat, an Olympian herself, is better known for coaching sprinter Evelyn Ashford.

The other Pat is a male with an *e* in his last name. Once a national-class 10,000-meter runner, this Connelly now coaches runners by the hundreds. He guides the L.A. Marathon Road Runners through six months of group training. He also oversees the Students Run L.A. program that prepares high school kids for the Los Angeles Marathon.

Separate groups meet with Connelly two nights a week at an area track. He's the longtime coach of the Basin Blues Club, and has worked with many high school and college teams.

Join a team or training group. Share in the pooled knowledge of other runners with similar abilities.

Yet coaching isn't his real job. Connelly serves with the Los Angeles Police Department—and of course coaches its running team.

"I get the same thrill enhancing people's lives through running as I do being a police officer," he told writer Jeff Green. "I'm serving the community."

Connelly added, "I had some great running instructors [notably Pete Petersons] when I ran competitively, and they were able to positively direct my energies toward athletics and life. It's rewarding to be able to share that knowledge with the public."

Coaches are scarce for today's runners, especially for the majority that isn't served by the traditional school-based coach. The quickest way to fill this void would be to develop more Pat Connellys—older runners who can share their wisdom with newer runners.

Every experienced runner is capable of coaching someone else. As the number of veteran runners grows, so does the pool of qualified coaches.

Any smart runner can be this type of coach. And any runner with a phone, a computer modem, a fax machine, or a mailbox can have one.

Become an informal coach. Pass along your lessons to someone who needs the support you once received.

This type of coach is a freelancer who often does his or her work without pay, as a favor to friends seeking advice. A few of these coaches are professionals, but almost none of them earns a full living this way.

He or she need not be a great runner to coach well. The best runners don't automatically make the best coaches, but many are blessed with both talents.

Fred Wilt stood as an early model for this type of coach. Once one of the country's top runners, he advised world-record marathoner Buddy Edelen by mail. Wilt also worked for a time with Hal Higdon, then a highly rated steeplechaser and marathoner and later a part-time coach himself.

Jeff Galloway, Benji Durden, and Ken Martin are 1990s versions of Wilt. Ex-Olympian Galloway coaches through clinics, camps, and magazine columns. Marathon Olympian Benji Durden coaches long-distance from Colorado. Martin, a sub-2:10 U.S. marathoner, has coached by fax machine.

Two-twelve marathoner Tom Fleming coaches from his running shop in New Jersey. Olympic steepler Mike Manley coaches a club team in

Oregon. Olympic champion Bob Schul has coached for years in Ohio, as have medalist Al Lawrence in Texas and early sub-four-minute miler Laszlo Tabori in California.

The pool of potential coaches widens and deepens as experienced runners look for ways to pass on all that they know. We can never have too many of them.

23

Better

Friends

My racing once took an ugly turn. The incident dates from the 1970s, but I still remember it too well.

At the end of a four-mile race, I heard footsteps and looked back. A boy was sprinting to catch me as his faster teammates cheered, "Don't let that old guy beat you!"

As the boy came up on my right side, I veered that way to fend him off. He chopped his stride and cut to the left, but I again blocked his path and still led him as our race ended.

Afterward the boy gasped, "That . . . was . . . a dirty trick . . . running me . . . off the road . . . like that." I agreed that it was and apologized.

A George Sheehan story had a happier ending. It was about competition at its best.

George was running the last mile of a race when he heard someone coming up from behind. As the younger man pulled alongside and then ahead, Sheehan called, "Way to go. You're looking great."

George didn't surrender meekly but recalled chasing the man as best he could. "Until he challenged me I had been running to survive, thinking I was doing the best I could. Now I discovered reserves I had not suspected were there. I finished with my best time of the year."

Such encounters, said Sheehan, are "the rule rather than a rarity in running. They embody the essence of the running experience.

"Nevertheless the younger man found my encouragement almost incomprehensible. The idea that an opponent would urge you to beat him seemed an impossibility. He became so psyched up, he said, that he ran better than he had thought possible."

This is competition at its best because you draw strength from other runners without draining any of theirs. You don't have to push anyone down to stand tall.

Sheehan said, "The Latin root of the word competition is *petere*—to go out, to head for, to seek. The *com* is doing it together, in common, in unity, in harmony. Competition, then, is simply each of us seeking our absolute best with the help of each other."

Wish your competitors well, said George, because "the better they do, the better [you] will do."

> View the other runners in your races as friends, not competitors. Cooperate with them to improve everyone's race.

Competing with them makes you run harder, longer, faster than you could go alone. In this setting Sheehan would find it "unthinkable to cheat anyone else or to be diminished by the performance of another." You feel no need to play physical or psychological tricks on your competitors.

This is the ideal way of viewing a race: runners all in it together, helping and not opposing one another, working as a team to accomplish common goals that each one of them might reach.

The reality of racing isn't quite this pure. But don't worry, sainthood isn't a qualification for entering races.

You aren't required to abandon all aggressive urges or to feel guilty about wanting to beat people to the finish line. Most racing falls somewhere between George Sheehan's example and mine.

You don't need to love your fellow racers as brothers and sisters, but don't get in their way, either. Follow the long-standing custom in distance racing of treating other runners with the same respect with which you expect to be treated.

Mind your manners, if for no other reason than self-interest. Interfere with someone else's race and yours could suffer too. Observe common courtesies or the race could dissolve into a street fight.

Teammate Friends

This race in Shreveport, Louisiana, had little to excite me and gave no hint that it would be one of my most memorable in years. I hadn't even planned to run the race before traveling there.

It wasn't a true running event, but more of a time trial, with each runner starting separately. It wasn't even a real triathlon, despite that billing.

The Fitness Fest Triathlon replaced the swim with a walk at the start. A walker, a biker, and a runner competed as a team, and two women— I knew them only as Jan and Gigi—recruited me for their 5K run. Our teamwork added an element that had been lacking from my racing for a long time.

For one who claims to be a loner—who trained apart from my high school and college teams, and who now runs alone 9 days of every 10— I still have a fondness for team racing. Spending so much time by myself makes the rare chances I have to work together all the more special.

Team up with friends. Train together for a big event. Travel there together. Run a relay race together.

Track never has seemed like much of a team sport. Only a common uniform links the whole track team. Milers and shot putters are as unrelated as swimmers and football players, and mixing their results in the scoring says little about a team's running talent.

Even the distance runners split into different events on the track. They really only team up for relays, and relay racing is my second-favorite type of race.

Cross-country comes first—as much for its teamwork as its terrain. Everyone runs the same race at the same time in cross-country, and individual runner's places are pooled for a team score that means something.

Relay and cross-country teamwork contributes heavily to my list of fondest memories. These memories don't center on what *I* did but on what *we* did:

- Running on the two-mile relay team my first season on track and being pulled all the way to the state meet.
- Winning the state cross-country team title the first season my school offered that sport, and again the next year.
- Scoring points for Drake University's three straight winning teams at the conference cross-country championships.
- Making Drake's team for the NCAA cross-country meet and sometimes its relay teams for major track meets—the only ways I ever could have raced on a national level.
- Competing in *Runner's World*'s first 24-hour relay for the company team.
- Circling Lake Tahoe as part of a group of strangers who became a team that day.

Even my worst memory of failure centers on a team race. South Page High School would win the state indoor track title if the medley relay team placed first.

My teammates handed me the baton within reach of the leaders to start the final half-mile leg. I focused on catching up little by little and forgot about everything else—including counting laps.

Coming off what seemed to be the last turn, I sprinted into the lead and triumphantly across the finish line. The triumph was short-lived.

An official shouted, "You aren't done yet. You stopped a lap too soon."

I stumbled the other lap. The team didn't place and didn't win the state title.

I've made other dumb mistakes in racing, but none has haunted me as this one did. Here, I didn't just make a fool of myself but also failed the three teammates who all had done their parts.

This story illustrates the two sides of teamwork. You get extra support from the team, but also carry extra responsibilities. Running for a team adds to the pre-race concern over letting your teammates down, but in turn it multiplies the post-race joy over your joint successes.

The worry makes you work harder. It's no accident that my PRs for both the outdoor and indoor mile came in relays—or that my fastest 5K in years came at the Shreveport 5K.

That triathlon brought back the old mixture of pre-race dread about failing the team and post-race joy at running better together than I would have alone. The nice twist in teamwork is that by giving more of yourself to the team, you get more from and for yourself in return.

Helping Friends

This isn't news you want to hear anytime, let alone at 5:30 the morning after an otherwise satisfying day. "The kid didn't make it," said Pete League as I joined him at breakfast.

The "kid" was 25-year-old Glenn Ewing, a trained marathoner capable of running well below three hours. He'd collapsed at the finish line of the Houston-Tenneco Marathon and had died overnight of what doctors described as "a rare affliction that resulted in massive internal bleeding."

Pete League had never met Ewing and didn't see him fall. But the news hit Pete like a death in the family. He felt somewhat responsible.

League had founded this race 20 years earlier. He now served as one of director David Hannah's most trusted assistants, taking charge of

© Photo Run/Robert Rinaldi

Experience the rewards of friendly competition and mutual accomplishment.

the finish area in and around a convention center—including the medical team.

Everything that could be done for the fallen runner was done. Help arrived within seconds, and he received the best emergency care.

League had gone three straight nights without much sleep, and his work wasn't finished yet. That Monday, he would collect statements from workers who'd witnessed the tragedy.

Pete handled his big job without asking for pay or fanfare. When we met on Saturday, he said, "I woke up at two o'clock this morning and couldn't get back to sleep. All these details were racing through my mind."

We met the day before raceday at the finish line, where he'd been since dawn and would stay until after dark—then awaken again at two o'clock on raceday morning, be at his post by five, and not leave until late Sunday afternoon.

While staying with Pete and his wife Lynn that weekend, I hung out more than usual at ground zero. Watching the finish area come together and then come down was something every runner should do.

Seeing it in Houston reminded me of several truths:

1. Running the race may be one of the easiest jobs done that day. At least it takes less time than the scene-setting work that starts well before the first runner arrives and ends long after the last one leaves.

2. Runners as a group are quick to complain and they're slow to thank the workers. They gripe if T-shirts aren't the right size or the bananas aren't ripe, then expect someone to clean up after them.

3. Runners are transients. They come and go like replaceable parts. Workers like Pete League are the permanent fixtures who keep these races running.

Being with Pete reminded me of an old plea. Runners would do well to practice a form of tithing.

For every 10 races that they run, they should agree to work at one. Hand out race numbers, work an aid station, stand on a corner and direct traffic, read mile splits, check in finishers, give away T-shirts, award the winners, or assist the injured.

Doing this would help a sport that's always long on runners and short on helpers. It would also help the runner become slower with the complaints and quicker with the compliments.

Few runners in Houston noticed Pete League at work on raceday, let alone thanked him for his help. But he hadn't taken this job for the applause.

Volunteer to work at 1 race for every
10 that you run. Give some of the
assistance you receive at other events.

Pete helped for the best of reasons. He had been a runner for 40 years and had received this kind of unsung assistance hundreds of times. Now graduated from his own racing, he gave back to others what he had so often gotten himself.

Remembering Friends

Amby Burfoot, my boss at *Runner's World*, came out my way to watch the Portland Marathon. At dinner before the race, he asked, "What brought you back to running marathons?"

"The better question is 'who,' " I said. "If I had to name one person, it would be Jeff Galloway. He showed me how to get to and through a marathon without destroying myself."

As a small and symbolic thank-you, I wore a T-shirt from Jeff's running camp in both of my marathons that year. The shirt choice matters when going this distance.

That spring, I returned to my ancestral running home for the last Drake Relays Marathon. What else could I wear but a Drake shirt?

Bob Williams greeted me first after one run in Portland. "See this?" I said, pointing to the soggy shirt from the marathon training program that he directs. That group had inspired me to enter this race, and this was my token of thanks.

During a talk that fall at the Royal Victoria Marathon, I told the runners on race eve, "Right now, you're thinking only about yourself and what you have to do tomorrow. That's to be expected, because running the marathon is completely your responsibility.

"But with your training finished and your race not yet here, why not take a little time today to think about someone besides yourself? You aren't alone in this effort, you know. There's a 'who' behind each one of you.

"Someone inspired, encouraged, or challenged you to try a marathon. Someone taught you how to train, trained with you, or supported your extra training. Think about it: Who's your 'who'?"

In Amby Burfoot's case, it was someone who cured him miraculously. "I suffered for seven years with a calf-muscle injury," said Amby in Portland.

He wanted to make the 25th anniversary of his Boston Marathon victory a respectable effort. But the calf problem left him limping from the halfway point on.

Soon afterward, he traveled to South Africa to help launch that country's edition of *Runner's World*. He met and was treated by a physiotherapist named Graeme Lindenberg.

"I felt so good," Amby said, "that I ran and finished the Comrades race. I felt only half a twinge in the whole 90K."

Lindenberg was his "who." Amby's run was a nine-hour thank-you to the therapist.

At your next big event, think about who made it possible. Show your appreciation to that person by dedicating the race to him or her.

You can do this graphically by printing a name on a shirt. The inscription might read "Running for Richard" or "In memory of Maria."

I saw many signs like this on the backs of runners at the Portland Marathon. Thoughtful as the gesture was, though, I'd never made it. My dedications were less formal but just as real.

At the Drake Relays, it was my parents. I'd lived with them during college at Drake, in houses along this course.

Dad and Mom had been here for the first Drake Marathon, 25 years earlier. He had since died, and she now faced cancer surgery (which would be successful). This was their race, too.

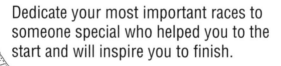

Dedicate your most important races to someone special who helped you to the start and will inspire you to finish.

At Portland, I ran with George Sheehan. He's a second father to me, and he was then climbing the toughest hill of his long illness. Thinking of him eased the miles after 20.

Run your next race for someone who can't be there in person. Wear a name on your shirt or just carry it in your heart.

24

Better

Thoughts

A little fear is good for you. Uncertainty about the outcome gets the competitive and creative juices flowing. But uncontrolled tension works at cross-purposes with racing. It can leave you physically drained and mentally devastated.

My first year in college, fear paralyzed me. I would fall apart in mid-race and either shuffle home or drop out.

The past and future frightened me. I feared not repeating the successes that had won me a college scholarship, and worried that the school would yank my free ride if I failed.

That problem corrected itself when I found a new scheme for financing college that didn't depend on race results. I could again finish the races I'd started.

Even now, though, a good memory and an active imagination

sometimes curse me when I face any big job. When lining up to race, standing up to speak, or sitting down to write, I fret over reliving old glories and avoiding new flops.

It's a common problem. Anyone who suffers from it would do well to heed that wonderfully blunt Nike slogan, "Just Do It."

Anyone who suffers too much from pre-race jitters (or panic attacks anytime) should get to know Dr. Herbert Benson. Read his book, and adopt its central practice.

Dr. Benson observed the effects of chronic tension while studying the causes and treatment of high blood pressure at the Harvard Medical School. He later prescribed a nonmedical antidote called "the relaxation response."

In a book by the same name, Benson simplified and demystified ancient techniques of meditation. He explained that his technique "is drawn with little embellishment from four basic components found in a myriad of historical methods. We claim no innovation but simply a scientific validation of age-old wisdom."

Those four elements are

1. a quiet setting with "as few distractions as possible,"
2. a mental focus such as "a repeated word or phrase to break the train of distracting thoughts,"
3. a passive mind kept that way by "repetition of the mental device," and
4. a comfortable position, "usually sitting because it keeps you from falling asleep."

Pre-event tension doesn't peak at the starting line or later, but before you start to warm up and release some of the pressure. It usually peaks when the body is idle, but the memory and imagination are most active.

Sit down and relax before races. Remember that your race is already 98 percent won when you reach the starting line.

If tension threatens to overwhelm you, let Dr. Benson's 10- to 20-minute routine relax you. His advice: "Sit quietly, and close your eyes.

Deeply relax all your muscles, beginning at your feet and progressing up to your face. Breathe through your nose, and become aware of your breathing."

With each breath, say to yourself the focusing word or phrase. I like "here and now," and use it to break the fixation on scary thoughts of there and then.

Loose Thoughts

Sitting down and relaxing before racing is a good start, wrote Jerry Lynch when Dr. Herbert Benson's advice appeared in a column of mine. Running relaxed, he went on to say, is even better.

Dr. Lynch, author of several sport psychology books, recommended another author's work—if you can find it. "Bud Winter's *Relax and Win* is a classic. I believe it's out of print, but his 80-percent rule remains a significant statement."

Winter's message needs telling and retelling. I last repeated it when he died at age 76 on the eve of his induction into the National Track and Field Hall of Fame.

Winter coached sprinters at San Jose State University—among them Lee Evans, Tommie Smith, and John Carlos. At the 1968 Olympics, Evans set a world 400-meter record that lasted for 20 years, and Smith won the 200 while breaking the mark held by Carlos (who placed third at Mexico City).

Their coach preached relaxation. He taught his athletes to race at what felt like less than full effort.

Winter said that trying to give—in the words of a long-running deodorant ad—"110 percent" is counterproductive. Excessive effort creates tension, which causes you to run with the brakes on.

"Relaxation leads to full efficiency of performing muscles," said Winter. "The thing you want is leg speed, and relaxation achieves this. Therefore to run at top speed you run with four-fifths effort."

The coach might have exaggerated by calling for 80-percent efforts from sprinters. He told them this so they wouldn't try to give 110 percent, and tie themselves in physical and emotional knots.

Winter learned this trick during World War II, while instructing student pilots. "We took guys who froze at the controls and made them the best fliers in the Navy," he wrote in his relaxation book.

He said that athletes are more likely to succeed by relaxing and letting their trained-in talent flow out than by straining and struggling to exceed themselves. "The key is learning to relax under pressure. An athlete who wants to do or die for good old Rutgers or San Jose State is as good as dead."

Relaxation is a first cousin of concentration. Relaxing means eliminating counterproductive motions. Concentrating means blocking out self-defeating thoughts.

"Don't confuse concentration with consternation," warned sport psychologist Dr. Scott Pengelly. Pengelly said that consternation results from trying too hard to make goals come true. Concentration involves tuning out such distractions.

Tom Miller, a student of both sport psychology and exercise physiology as well as a coach and marathoner, once illustrated for me the difference between these two approaches. He played a videotape from the 1985 Chicago Marathon, featuring women's leaders Ingrid Kristiansen and Joan Samuelson.

Kristiansen had made no secret of wanting to be the first woman to break 2:20 after coming within 66 seconds of that barrier earlier in the year. Samuelson, whose best time going into the Chicago race was 2:22:43, hadn't expressed any time goal.

On the tape, Ingrid wore a look of consternation as she glanced alternately at how her splits compared with goal pace and at the woman she had to beat. Joan seemed serene by comparison, concentrating entirely on what she herself was doing and feeling.

Samuelson looked unconcerned about either pace or place, yet held better control of each than if she'd overreached for 110-percent effort. She ran her own fastest marathon of 2:21:21 that day, and beat the harder-trying but tighter world-record holder.

Inspired Thoughts

Reading running magazines should be inspiring, not intimidating. But if we're not careful, these stories can psych us out instead of up.

We read about the times and training of great runners and wonder, "How much are my little efforts worth?"

Tiny pangs of inferiority struck twice while I read one issue of *Runner's World*. Each time, a single line in a long feature article was to blame.

Steve Scott, the miler, wrote of his warm-up routine in college: "Every day without fail, we'd do 30 to 40 minutes of jogging and stretching before our workout."

Take information and inspiration from big-name athletes. But don't let their amazing stories intimidate you.

Don Kardong, the ex-Olympic marathoner, wrote about weight-loss workouts: "An interval or steady run of an hour or more may induce the largest rise [in calorie burning]."

My efforts look puny by these standards. Thirty to 40 minutes of easy running and stretching often *is* my workout. I rarely go longer than an hour and never run any intervals.

© Photo Run/Victor Sailer

Gathering thoughts—Arturo Barrios before the 1993 New York Marathon.

Reading puts me at twice the risk of psych-out. As a runner and a writer, both the running content and the writing style of articles might intimidate me.

Kardong's way with words could have the latter effect. The work of Don, Kenny Moore, John Brant, and other running writers might make me wonder, "Why try to do what they already do so much better?" if I hadn't learned how to deal with these doubts.

"Writer's block," the most dreaded disease of story-makers, is misnamed. It really should be called *"reader's* block."

Reading the work of better writers, then trying and failing to meet their standards, is one cause. Feeling the unseen eyes of readers over your shoulder, judging your phrases "not good enough," is another.

These failures paralyze the flow of ideas. Because you can't be a Steinbeck, you're tempted to stop doing anything.

I can't stop writing. For one thing, that would mean stopping eating or starting a new career.

So when the first symptoms of a blockage appear, I remind myself what type of writer I am and am not. I'm a reporter (a repeater of other people's words) and a journalist (in the truest sense of that word—a keeper of journals).

My job is to keep writing—to fill a journal page every day, a newsletter and a magazine column each month, a book every few years. To keep the writing flowing, I follow three simple rules: (1) find a subject that excites you; (2) write about it as best you can; and (3) be proud of the result, knowing that a better writer couldn't have written it for you.

"Runner's block" has similar causes, symptoms, and cures. It starts with reading about the sport's giants, measuring yourself against them, and falling short.

Run the best you can with the talent you have and the training you've done, and you can call yourself a winner.

The ailment worsens when you try and fail to run as the giants do. You judge your efforts, or feel them being judged, as "not good enough."

Failure may paralyze the flow of your running. If you can't be an Alberto Salazar or a Joan Samuelson, you wonder, "Why try to do what they already do so much better?" And you're tempted to stop trying to do anything.

You can't afford to stop. So at the first sign of blockage, think about who you are and aren't as a runner.

You'll probably never go to the Olympics, set American records, or earn your living as a runner. Once you accept these facts, you can relax and get on with your work.

Your job is to keep running. To keep up the flow, follow three simple rules:

- *Run for yourself.* You only need to judge yourself against your-self.
- *Run what you can.* Anything you run is better than running noth-ing.
- *Be proud of your runs.* Lots of people go longer and faster, but none could have done your work for you.

Now you can read for inspiration.

Lasting Thoughts

I'm undereducated in the formal sense. My schooling ended with a liberal arts degree and a social science major that left me unprepared to teach and coach in high school as originally planned, or for any other job except the one I've had since graduation.

Drake University's catalog didn't list running as a major. But this became my unofficial course of study.

I ran on Drake's team, traveled to nearly half the states, wrote about those meets for the school paper, and devoured the work of running writers. This would be the best possible training for what I'd do later.

> Savor the practical lessons that run-ning teaches—such as the natural pace of life being less than 10 miles an hour.

Running taught me—and still teaches me—more than I'd otherwise know about subjects from geography to meteorology, from physiology to podiatry. Robert Fulghum wrote a great little book about learning everything he needed to know in kindergarten. I'm not threatening to steal his theme for a book on running's lessons, but the subject does at least merit part of a chapter.

Running teaches all of us in ways we never suspected at the time of enrollment. Consider these lessons, for instance:

- You learn to say "fartlek" without laughing. And to wear rainbow-colored tights without fear of being laughed at.

- You learn to load up on cheap, starchy foods without guilt. You call them "fuel."

- You learn to justify drinking beer as "fluid replacement." You think of coffee as a "performance booster."

- You learn to talk in numbers that are understood only by other runners. You speak a little metric, but not well enough to understand it without converting distances back to miles.

- You learn to wear sensible shoes for all occasions. Your running shoes serve many other purposes.

- You learn to spit in public. And to make pitstops without going indoors. And to blow your nose with thumb and forefinger.

- You learn to walk bare-legged and sweaty into a hotel elevator filled with people dressed for business. You gain a little more appreciation for how the homeless are made to feel all the time.

- You learn to endure questions like "How long is this week's marathon?" Or "You look so skinny; have you been sick?"

- You learn that a cool, gray, damp day that isn't much good for anything else can be a great day to run. An empty place which serves no other recreational purpose can be a great place for running.

- You learn how the "quarter-mile rule" works. Very few people will travel on foot more than a quarter-mile from a parking lot, so you can quickly run away from crowds.

- You learn that the natural pace for a human being to travel is less than 10 miles per hour, not 55 and above. You realize that your first source of energy doesn't flow through a gas pump.

- You learn to read the sports section from the back forward, checking for scraps of news about your sport. You learn to read the fine-print cable listings in the TV guide, then to program the VCR for taping odd-hour showings of running events.

- You finally learn to heed the advice your mother once gave you: Get your rest, eat your vegetables, don't exercise for an hour after eating, remember to take your vitamins, and wear clean shorts in case you must go to the hospital.

- You learn to ignore as an adult the other warnings Mom gave you in childhood. You're now free to go out in the rain, to get your shoes muddy, to stay out after dark, and to play in the street.

25

Better

Years

I've been a tireless traveler since joining the running circuit decades ago. For a few days every few weeks, I go to places great and small. And while there, I visit nothing more than an airport, a meeting hall, and a race course.

Robert Louis Stevenson wrote, "I travel not to go anywhere, but to go." I travel not to sightsee, but to *people*-see.

I must get away from home and go where runners gather. I need to travel to see whom I'm writing for, what they're talking about and hoping to read. I want to travel to see fellow runners not just as readers but as friends.

I usually see them only as they are now, which is fine. Sometimes, though, a runner walks up, introduces himself, and pulls out an old driver's license photo. It shows someone who looks heavier, older, and wearier than the person standing here now.

"This is how I looked before I started running five years ago," he says proudly. The obvious goes unsaid: He would still look that way, or worse, if he hadn't become a runner.

Running changed his life. I admire him for changing so much and envy him for having such clear before and after pictures of himself.

Ask yourself, "What would I be now if I hadn't become a runner?" The later in life your start came, the easier it is to answer. You know where you were headed before changing directions.

I can't answer that question. I started running as a kid of 14, never stopped, and know no other way but this one.

I couldn't have guessed what was beginning on April Fool's Day 1958. I can't imagine how different life would have been on another course.

That first race led to another, then more—until the total reached hundreds. One mile led to two, then three, then six—and on to the marathon and beyond. Local racing led to ever-widening circuits that this country's borders wouldn't be big enough to hold.

Take as much pleasure in revisiting old places repeatedly as you once did in exploring them for the first time.

Running taught me to read and write. It determined where I went to college and what I studied there.

Running gave me all of my jobs, from the first one to my current one. It mapped the places where I've lived and traveled. It made possible the friendships formed and the family started.

Running shaped how I look, think, and act. More than any other force except heredity, running made me who I am.

I can't imagine being anyone else, or wanting to be. I'm too busy being happy with what *is* to speculate about "What if . . . ?"

Lasting Years

"Last" is a four-letter word only when it appears after "dead." The track writer for my local paper persists in using that combination.

I cringe each time he writes "dead last." He makes the runner occupying that spot—usually someone good enough to make one of the toughest college teams in the country—sound like roadkill.

Words matter. The labels we attach to ourselves and one another shape attitudes.

I'd just begun stringing together words about running when I wrote an article that called runners "addicts," "fanatics," and "masochists." It was meant to be funny.

Bob Karnes, my college track coach, didn't see the humor. "If you call yourself these names," he said, "how can you expect anyone who doesn't run to think otherwise?"

I've rarely used words of weirdness since then. Enough people already think we're oddballs without our agreeing with them.

Now that I write, teach writing, and edit other writers, I'm more aware than ever of how words play on the mind. Some annoy (referring to shoes as "sneakers" and race numbers as "bibs" as if preschoolers were wearing them), some demean (calling someone an "also-ran," or

© F-Stock/John Laptad

Better your running for the life-long run.

worse, a "jogger"), and some confuse (what do "fun run" and "minimara-thon" really mean?).

Some words speak volumes about our views of runners and running. Notice how warlike words pollute sports talk.

One athlete or team doesn't just "beat" another. One "crushes," "guns down," "blows away," or "destroys" the other.

Hard-work words also infect all sports. Where would we be without our "workouts"? Maybe better off.

When I was a boy just starting to run in Iowa, Ames High School won all the state titles—but not by working harder than anyone else. In fact, these runners never heard their coach speak of "working out."

Hi Covey refused to use this name for training. He said, " 'Work' is a dreary word that calls up negative images. If I talked all the time about how hard running is, who would want to do it?"

Bill Bowerman coached hundreds of winning runners. Yet the former University of Oregon coach never uttered the ugly words "pain equals gain."

Bowerman aimed to move his athletes beyond thinking of training as a term of hard labor. "A banker friend of mine told me that he doesn't feel he has 'worked' a day in his life because he enjoys banking so much," the coach said. "A banker must practice banking virtually 12 months a year.

"Runners must do the same with their running. If they don't do that and don't enjoy it, they're never going to reach the top.

"Well, they may not reach the top anyway. But if they enjoy the running, they are getting one of its big prizes."

Even if they finish last.

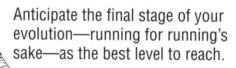

Anticipate the final stage of your evolution—running for running's sake—as the best level to reach.

Coming Years

In my neighborhood, I see the future of running every day. It looks great. The gloomy forecasts you might have read about this being a dying "fad" are flat wrong.

Eugene is the country's original mass-running center, and I live near its heart. The favorite gathering place of the natives is the Amazon Trail, a one-mile sawdust path squeezed into its long, narrow shape by a creek (really more of a ditch) on one side and a heavily traveled street on the other.

This is one of the few trails in the country built for running and used almost entirely for that purpose, not for hiking, or biking, or horseback riding. Oh, how the runners use it!

I don't always run at Amazon, but do pass by daily to see who's out. Almost never is it empty. At peak hours of the early morning and late afternoon, the trail almost needs signal lights to control its human traffic.

The best part of running here, besides the spongy surface, is the star-gazing. Eugene has been at least the temporary home to some of the country's best-known runners, including Alberto Salazar and Mary Slaney. Watching these athletes when they're dressed casually, or are sleepy-eyed, or are limping, makes them seem more like the rest of us than when they're performing in races.

Mostly, though, this is where the common folk anonymously put in their miles for their private reasons. Most of them have no goal more grand than to run the same distance at the same time as yesterday, and to do the same again tomorrow.

If you visit Amazon regularly, you see the same faces week after month after year. They are the runners of the future. What has happened with them will happen with others, here and elsewhere.

Running came to Eugene, grew up, and matured earlier than it did in the rest of the country. The sport has evolved further here than in other places.

A runner typically passes through stages of evolution: from exerciser working to get back in shape, to racer training to improve times, to runner who runs just to be running. The sport as a whole seems to be moving in the same direction.

The dominant theme of the early running-boom years was fitness. It now is competition. It may evolve to lower-key recreational running.

Eugene was ahead of the times. Bill Bowerman started the town exercising in the 1960s, a decade earlier than boom times struck elsewhere.

Long-distance racing passed its peak here several years ago, and the city's major marathon—the Nike-Oregon Track Club—folded in 1984. Yet yesterday's marathoners haven't faded away. They still show up at Amazon.

This is not to say there are no new exercisers in Eugene. Kids from the university and adults from the nearby YMCA still flock to the trail.

And this isn't to say no one trains to race. Bill Dellinger's and Tom Heinonen's University of Oregon teams use Amazon. So do the athletes coached by Dick Brown, Mike Manley, and Alberto Salazar, and those from the local high schools and the Track City Track Club.

And I don't mean to say that Stage Three runners like me aren't concerned with fitness or that we never race. We just choose to do more running than the minimum requirements of exercise, and less than needed for high performance. We no longer run as if our lives and times depended upon it.

We now run mainly to keep running. That's the future you're promised, the one that is working just fine on the Amazon Trail.

Fresh Years

He was one of the first modern runners I ever met. Bob Carman ran as an adult, primarily on the roads, and as a way of life.

Carman, a 2:22 marathoner, was then a college professor in his early 30s. At 20, I wondered about his secret for running at such an advanced age but didn't dare ask at the time.

Years later, while compiling a booklet called *Road Racers and Their Training*, I finally asked. "How do you avoid getting bored with your running?" was how the questionnaire read.

Other runners gave specific and sometimes detailed answers. Carman simply wrote, "I've never found running boring."

His line comes back to me whenever I hear the tiresome refrain that running is a bore. It appeared recently in my hometown newspaper.

Measure the ultimate success of your career by the years and decades run, not by the minutes and seconds of your PRs.

A recreation writer took a swipe at one form of running to promote another. His story dealt with the serious fun-havers of the Hash House Harriers, who call themselves "drinkers with a running problem."

He wrote, "Do you feel your running life getting a little boring? Are you finding yourself stuck in the same rut, running the same route, with little or no variation, time after time?

"If you're like many people, your running routines probably fall into the 'same time, same station' pattern like that comforting yet bland feeling you get from watching the same old reruns on TV."

Observers of running, former runners, and even some minimalist runners will nod in agreement. They'll tell you, "I never run/used to run/only run a little because it's so-o-o bor-r-ring."

The nonrunner mistakes our look of concentration for boredom. The lapsed runner, who worked too hard while still unfit, mistakes discomfort for boredom. The casual runner, who stops after a mile or two, mistakes this warm-up (which can be mildly uncomfortable or, yes, boring) for real running (which starts where this person stops).

People who talk the most about this being a boring activity are those who run the least, or not at all. Those who run the most use this word the least, if ever.

Kenny Moore, who held the American marathon record at the time, did use the word in my *Road Racers* book. But he viewed this condition as one that could work to his benefit.

"Training is supposed to get one used to fatigue and boredom," Moore wrote, "so on hard days I sometimes deliberately choose boring routes to see how tired I can make myself."

Remember your first and foremost goal: to endure, to continue, to survive, to keep running, to finish last.

Certain of Moore's runs might have qualified as boring. But his running as a whole could not have been. Otherwise he wouldn't have taken it so far: two Olympic marathons, including a fourth-place finish, along with his U.S. record.

My running hasn't taken me far. But it has kept me touring the neighborhood for a long time.

I'm a "same time–same station" runner. I run the same handful of routes repeatedly, usually at the same hour.

I find the sameness of this routine to be comforting. Yet the runs themselves don't have the feel of "old reruns on TV."

They are as different from each other as snowflakes or fingerprints. No two ever combine their details in exactly the same way.

Weather changes from day to day and light conditions from season to season. Energy and motivation levels dictate changes in pace.

People passed, places seen, and things thought all change with each run.

Each run combines the familiarity of a routine with the surprises of a new day. This mix leaves no room for boredom.

Index

A

Adrenaline, on race day, 141, 146
Aerobic capacity, 123
Aerobic energy, 35
Aerobic fitness, 113, 122-125
Age
    impact on performance, 62-65
    impact on recovery rates, 41-43
    impact on running schedule, 39
    and race records, 79
Age-Graded Tables (WAVA), 63, 64-65
Aggression, 157-158
Alamo's Alumni races, 150
Allergies, 187-188
Almquist, Gary, 13
Alumni races, 150
Amazon Trail (Eugene, Oregon), 93, 235-236
Anderson, Bob ("Stretch"), 29
Anderson, Curtis, 206
Anderson, Owen, 131, 139-140, 142
Aqua Ark, 136
Ashford, Evelyn, 210
Athletic drinks, 190
Atkins, Orville, 187-188
Atlanta, Olympic Games in, 90
Avenue of the Giants (race), 147, 148
Awards, 158-162

B

Bacheler, Jack, 156, 208
Baker, Erin, 128-129
Barcelona, Olympic Marathon in, 90
Barrios, Arturo, 225
Basin Blues Club, 210
Bass, Eric, 136
Bee-pollen pitch, 186
Benoit, Joan. *See* Samuelson, Joan Benoit
Benson, Herbert, 222-223
Benson, Tony, 197-198
Bicycling (magazine), 94
Big sport, 157
Bike lanes and trails, 92, 94
Blakeslee, Sandra, 129
Body weight, 121
Books for Runners (booksellers), 183
Boston Marathon

    course of, 90
    drinking water at, 191
    1994 times in, 66
    weather conditions at, 102
Bowerman, Bill, 206-207, 208, 234, 235
Brant, John, 226
British Track and Field Literature, 1275 to 1968, 182
Brown, Dick, 117-122, 123, 124-125, 135-136, 236
B-rrry Scurry (Clinton, Iowa), 104
Buerkle, Dick, 113
Burfoot, Amby, 14, 200, 219-220
Butwell, Mike, 38
Butwin, David, 159

C

Caffeine, 190-192
Carbohydrate reloading, 45
Carbohydrate starvation, 186
Carbon dioxide, 36
Carlos, John, 223
Carman, Bob, 236
CBS (challenging, but safe) test, 119-121
Cedar Rapids, Iowa, bikepaths in, 94
Cedarwinds (booksellers), 183
Cerutty, Percy, xiv
Chacarito, Cerrildo, 169
Chadwick, Cheryl, 36
Chicago Marathon, female runners in, 224
Christensen, Roger, 196
Churro, Victoriano, 169-170
Cimons, Marlene, 112
Clark, Johnny, 167-168
Clarke, Ron, xiv, 154
Clayton, Derek, 5, 9
Climate
    dressing appropriately when traveling, 97
    and weather conditions, 99-106, 148
Clothing
    appropriate to climate/weather, 97
    high-tech fabrics in, 176
Coaching, 203-212
Coghlan, Eamonn, 62, 63
Cold, common, 199-200

Cold weather, running in, 102-105
Collapse-point theory, 54
Competition, 213-215, 235
Concentration, 224
Connelly, Pat, 138, 210-211
Connolly, Pat, 210
Conversations (Brown), 119
Converse shoe company, 170
Cool-down
    in interval training, 32
    stretching during, 130, 131
    walking as part of, 30
Cooper, Kenneth, 113, 115, 122-123, 196
Corporate races, 150
Costill, David, 35, 44, 46
Covert, Debi, 38
Covert, Mark, 37-38, 39
Covey, Hi, 234
Croghan, Mark, 106
Cross-country racing, 216
Cross-training
    bicycling as, 133-135
    as partial rests, 40-41
    on rotation schedule, 53
    skepticism about, 127-129
    for strength, 132-133
    swimming as, 135-136
    and three-day cycles, 50-51
    walking as, 30-31, 41
Cruise intervals, 110-111
Cures. *See* Medication

D

Daniels, Jack, 30, 110, 115
Daws, Ron, 169
Decker, Mary. *See* Slaney, Mary Decker
Dehydration, 186
Dellinger, Bill, 235
Detroit Free Press, 89
Diary. *See* Journal, recording in
Diet
    fads in, 185-186
    and food allergies, 187-188
    liquid, 190-192
    low-fat, 188-190
    solid, 192-194
    tolerance of, 187-189
Distance running
    of honest distances, 87-88
    of "junk" distances, 82, 83-84
    long, slow distance, 81-83
    of minimum distances, 84-87
    walking for, 33-35

Drinking, during races, xv, 145, 190-192
Drugs. *See* Medication
Durden, Benji, 211
Dwight, Jim, 89

E

Easy days, 7. *See also* Rests
Eating. *See also* Diet
    after races, 45
    before races, xv
    during races, 192-194
Edelen, Buddy, 211
Elliott, Herb, xiv, 3
Ellis, Joe, 166, 195-196
Endurance
    role of, 4
    as a runner, 231-238
    walking breaks for, 8, 12, 17-18, 31-33,
        50, 145, 191
Englehart, Richard, 22
Equipment, for triathalons, 176-178
Eugene, Oregon, hiking trails in, 93, 235-236
Evans, Lee, 223
Ewing, Glenn, 217
Eyewear, 180-181

F

Farmer, Jim, 208-209
Fast runs, 7. *See also* Pacing; Timing
Fifth Season 8K (Cedar Rapids, Iowa), 141
Financial rewards, 158-159
Finke, Warren, 84-85
Fitness, aerobic, xv, 113, 122-125, 235, 236
Fitness Fest Triathlon (Shreveport,
        Louisiana), 215
Fitness Running (Brown), 119, 121, 123
5K races
    popularity of, 114-115
    predicting pace of, 125-126
Fleming, Tom, 211
Flexibility, 130-131
Florida Track Club, 208
Food. *See* Diet
Fort Edmonton 5K, divisions of, 115
Foster, Jack, 9-10, 23-24, 115
Friedman, Meyer, 14
Friendship, 213-220
Fulghum, Robert, 228
Fun runs, 114

G

Galloway, Jeff
    and bicycling, 94

as a coach, 149, 211
counting strategy of, 54, 125
eating strategy of, 193-194
as inspiration, 219
resting and running strategy of, 12, 19-
20, 30, 49-51, 52
Gammoudi, Mohamed, 154
Gamow, Igor, 166
George, Walter, 144
Gilbert, Bil, 156-158
Gilmour, John, 79
Glucose pills, 190, 192
Goals
and fitness, 123, 235, 236
for improvement, 7-8
projections for, 59-61
for recovery, 4-6, 197-202
for survival, 8-10, 231-238
Goretex, 176
Green, Jeff, 211
Griffith, Florence. *See* Joyner, Florence
Griffith (FloJo)
Guthrie, Woody, 138

H
Hannah, David, 217
Harvey, Rex, 205
Hash House Harriers, 236
"Havelok the Dane," 182
Headsets, 176
Heart rate, 121
Heat, running in, 101-102, 148
Heinonen, Tom, 235
Henderson, Barbara, 21, 73
Henderson, Eric, 66, 132
Higdon, Hal, 51, 52, 79, 99, 100, 113-114, 211
High sport, 157
Hill, Jim, 179-180
Hill, Ron, xiv, 37, 38, 39, 179
Honolulu Marathon, 101
Hood-to-Coast Relay (Oregon), 150
Hot weather, running in, 101-102, 148
Houston-Tenneco Marathon, 217
How They Train (Wilt), 113
Humility, 147-148
Huntsville Track Club News, 161
"Hurry" sickness, 14
Hydration. *See* Dehydration; Drinking

I
Igloi, Mihaly, 187
Ikangaa, Juma, 78
Improvement goals, 7-8

Individual Trainer (handheld computer),
118, 119
Injuries
caused by mistakes, 130
cures for, 195-199
from overstretching, 131-132
prevention of. *See* Safety
and recovery goals, 4-6
rehabilitation from, 133
as trauma, 130
walking during recovery from, 30
walking to prevent, 30, 36, 129-131
Inside Running (Costill), 35
Inspiration
practical, 227-229
and relaxation, 221-224
remembering running friends for, 219-
220
sources of, 224-227
Interval training, 30, 31-33, 110-111, 113-114

J
James, Stan, 19, 197-199
Jasper-to-Banff Relay, 150
Jennings, Lynn, 106
Jet lag, 97
Jimmy Stewart Relay, 150
Johnston, Norm, 205
Jones, Kim, 106
Journal, recording in, 55-57
Joyner, Florence Griffith (FloJo), 177-178
"Junk" distances, 82, 83-84
Junren, Ma, 185-186
Junxia, Wang, 142-143

K
Kardong, Don, 225, 226
Karnes, Bob, 233
Kelley, Johnny, 3-4, 10, 151
Kennedy, Bob, 201-202
Kidder, Lew, 177
King, Karl, 35
Klein, Jeffrey, 158, 159
Kleinerman, Joe, xiii
Kosloff, Ed, 182
Kristiansen, Ingrid, 224
Kuipers, Harm, 140

L
L.A. Marathon Road Runners, 138, 210
Lactic acid, 36
Lakey, Donald, 81
Lally, David, 131

Lawrence, Al, 212
Leadville (Colorado) 100-miler, 169
League, Lynn, 218
League, Pete, 217-219
Lee, Ken, 131
Legs, products for, 178-180
Lemmon, Mark, 176
Letko, Anne Marie, 106
Levinson, Philip, 209
Lindenberg, Graeme, 220
Lindgren, Gerry, 154
Liquid diets, 190-192
Liquori, Marty, 190
Long, Slow Distance: The Humane Way to Train
　　(Henderson), xv, 82
Long Distance Log (magazine), xiii, 81
Long runs, 7, 83-84. *See also* Distance run-
　　ning
Lopes, Carlos, 7
Lore of Running (Noakes), 35
Los Altos Hills, California, fun runs in, 95
Los Angeles Marathon, 138
Low-fat diets, 188-190
LSD (Henderson), xv
Lumian, Norm, 182
Lycra, 176
Lydiard, Arthur, xiv, 12, 15, 78, 113, 169,
　　192-193, 206
Lynch, Jerry, 223

M

Mah, Sy, 151
Manley, Mike, 207-208, 211-212, 236
Manly Exercises, 182
Marathons
　　and interval training, 33
　　scheduling for, 53-54
　　strategy for survival in, 34-35, 85-87
　　tapering prior to, 139-141
　　three parts of, 88
　　training for, 53-54, 85-88
Maree, Sydney, 201
Martin, Ken, 208, 211
Masterpieces (magazine), 83
Masters running, 41-43
Masters Running and Racing (Rodgers and
　　Welch), 41, 202
Matson, Shirley, 62
Maximal oxygen uptake, 122-125
McFadden, James, 36
McKay, Jim, 190
Measurements
　　in metric units, 57-59

and one-mile test, 125-126
Meat eating, xv
Medals, 158-162
Medication
　　and cold cures, 199-200
　　and medical cures, 197-199
　　and rest cures, 201-202
Melby, Kathy, 189-190
Mental toughness, 157
Metaphors, 232-234
Metric measurements, 57-59
Meyer, Bill, 41, 43
Meyer, Maureen, 43
Mile speed. *See* Per-mile speed
Miller, Bob, 104
Miller, Tom, 134-135, 188-189, 224
Mills, Billy, 153-154, 155
Minimum speed, 112-114
Molina, Scott, 128
Moore, Kenny, 206-207, 208, 226, 237
Moran, Gary, 134
Morceli, Noureddine, 144
Morrison, Jerry, 83
Motivation
　　and pacing, 142-144
　　post-race, 139-141
　　and pride, 138-139
　　and warm-up, 141-142
Motor City Striders, 182
Mtolo, Willie, 190
Murray, Bill, 115
Muscle strength, 132-133, 134

N

National Fitness Trail, 94
National Masters News, 59, 64
Nenow, Mark, 25-27, 129
New Balance shoe company, 170
Newhams, Ken, 56
Newton, Arthur, xiii
New York City Marathon, 78
New York Road Runners Club, 150
Nike-Oregon Track Club, 235
Nike shoe company, 4, 206, 209
Noakes, Tim, 35
Nurmi, Paavo, 3
Nutrition. *See* Diet

O

Ogilvie, Bruce, 156, 157
Ohio Runner, 176
One-mile test, 125-126
One-pace-runner syndrome, 111-112

Orthopedic problems, 195
Osler, Tom, 12, 18, 142, 145, 169, 191
Out-and-back courses, 90-91, 97
Out-of-town courses, 96-98

P

Pacing. *See also* Timing
    faster, 75-76
    versus fitness, 123
    in marathons, 86
    and one-mile test, 125-126
    record-setting, 78-79
    slower, 73-74, 111-112
    and speed, 107-115
    tactics for, 142-144
    truer, 76-77
Pain, during training, xv, 9
Pengelly, Scott, 224
Performance
    impact of age on, 62-65
    metric results of, 57-58
    and personal records, 65-67
    products to enhance, 176-178
    projections for, 59-61
    safe levels of, 122
    written results of, 56-57
Per-mile speed, 111-112
Personal library, 182-183
Personal records (PR)
    goals after achieving, 9
    and performance goals, 65-67
    and winning, 72
Personal rewards, 156-158
Petersons, Pete, 211
Plaatjes, Mark, 106
Podkopayeva, Yekaterina, 63
Polypropylene, 176
Portland Marathon, 150
Post, Marty, 182
Post-marathon blues, 46
Post-race rest and recovery, 44-46, 139-141
Powerbars, 193-194
PR. *See* Personal records (PR)
Pre-race rest, 43-44
Pre's Trail (Eugene, Oregon), 93
Pritikin, Nathan, 189
Prokop, Dave, 132-133

Q

Quarter-mile rule, 228
Quota system, 48, 54

R

Race courses, 78-79, 89-98

Race records, 79
Racewalking, 30, 36
Racing
    competition in, 213-215
    counting races entered, 151-152
    course variety in, 78-79, 89-98
    eating during, 192-194
    and humility, 147-148
    quality of races, 78
    resting before and after, 43-46, 139-141, 147
    resting between races, 8, 12, 17, 18-20,
        37-46, 51, 209-210
    runners' longevity in, 79
    speed during, 114-115
    strategies for, 145-152
    as training, 12, 15-17
    training for, xv
    trends in, 148-150
Rails to Trails Conservancy, 94
Ratelle, Alex, 35-36
Recordkeeping, journal for, 55-57
Recovery goals, 4-6
Recovery rates, 41-43, 46
Recreational running, 235
Reese, Paul, 91, 94
References, 182-183
Rehabilitation, 133
Relax and Win (Winter), 223
Relaxation, 221-224
Relay races, 150, 215-216
Rests
    alternating with running, 8, 12, 17, 18-
        20, 51, 209-210
    as cures, 201-202
    earning, 39-40
    masters, 41-43
    partial, 40-41
    post-race, 44-46, 139-141, 147
    pre-race, 43-44, 139-141
Results. *See* Goals; Performance
Rewards, versus winning, 153-162
Rhoden, William C., 186
Road Racers and Their Training (Henderson),
        236, 237
Road Runners' Club of America, 161
Rodgers, Bill, 41, 43, 125, 202, 208
Roe, Dean, 12, 203-205
Ross, Browning, 81
Rotating schedule, 51-53
Run for the Cure, 114
"Runner's block," 226
Runner's World (magazine), xiv, 14, 94, 111,
        113, 132, 158, 182, 209, 224

Running: A Guide to the Literature (Post and Wischnia), 182
Running program, components of, 7
Running Research News, 131, 139, 142
Running shoes. *See* Shoes
Running streaks, 37-40

S

Safety
    and reading body signs, 118, 119, 121, 122-125
    of running in cold weather, 102-105
    on street courses, 91-92
    during training, 119-121, 133
    of triathlons, 177-178
    while traveling, 97
Saigon squat, 29
Salazar, Alberto, 25, 125, 202, 208-210, 235, 236
Samuelson, Joan Benoit, 5-6, 25, 190, 202, 224
Scheduling
    around weather conditions, 105-106
    daily versus weekly, 48
    impact of age on, 39
    marathon schedule, 53-54
    and quota system, 48, 54
    rotating schedule, 51-53
    three-day schedule, 49-51, 52
Schul, Bob, 212
Schwane, James A., 129-130
Scott, Steve, 224
Seasons. *See* Climate; Weather
Selye, Hans, 119
Serious Runner's Handbook (Osler), 18, 191
Setnes, Kevin, 35
Shared courses, 95-96
Sheehan, George
    and competition, 213-214
    and distance running, 83, 85-86
    and earning your shower, 40
    as inspiration, 220
    and race counting, 151
    and racing speed, 114
    and reasons for running, 113, 137
    resting and racing strategy of, 19
    and treating injuries and illness, 188-189, 199, 200
Sheehan, George, III, 185
Shoes
    cost of, 165-167
    development of, 175-176
    modification of, 169-171

retirement of, 171-173
rotation of, 52, 167-169
Shorter, Frank, 125, 155-156, 190, 208
Sightseeing, while running, 98
Single-loop courses, 90-91
Slaney, Mary Decker, 4-5, 6, 25, 118, 120, 135-136, 202, 235
Sleep, 121
Slovut, Gordon, 36
Smith, John, 208
Smith, Les, 148
Smith, Tommie, 223
Socializing, 149, 150
Speed. *See also* Pacing; Timing
    minimum, 112-114
    per mile, 111-112, 125-126
    during racing, 114-115
    on tracks, 108-111
Spivey, Jim, 106
SportHill clothing company, 179-180
Sports bars, 193
Sports Illustrated, 157, 159
Sportsmanship, 213-215
Sports medicine, 197-199
Springbocs, 166-167
Spring Classic (Portland, Oregon), 208-209
Stack, Walt, 112
Stahl, Kjell-Erik, 101
Stampfl, Franz, xiii
Steely, Shelly, 118
Stevenson, Robert Louis, 231
St. Geme, Ceci, 190
Stopwatches, 66, 71-73, 176
Story, Dale, 206
Street courses, 91-92
Strength. *See* Muscle strength
Stress management, 119, 221-224
Stretching, 108, 129-132
Stretch reflex, 132
Students Run L.A. program, 210
Sugar, 190-192
Survival goals, 8-10, 231-238
Swimming, 135-136

T

Tabori, Laszlo, 212
Tale of the Ancient Marathoner (Foster), 23
Tartan track weatherproofing, 175
Teammates, 215-217
Tellez, Tom, 208
Temperature. *See* Climate; Weather
Tempo runs, 110
Tendrich, Eugenie, 158-159

Ten Million Steps (Reese), 91
Thomas, Doug, 195
Thoughts and inspiration, 221-229
Three-day schedule, 49-51, 52
Time-running, 15
Time zones, 97
Timing. *See also* Speed
  and course variety, 78-79
  versus fitness, 123
  and race quality, 78
  and runners' longevity, 79
  with stopwatches, 66, 71-73
  in training, 12, 14-15
Tinsley, Harold, 161
Tough-mindedness, 157
"Tow method," xiv
Track and Field News, 40
Track City Track Club, 236
Track speed, 108-111
Track Technique (magazine), xiv
Trail courses, 93-95
Training. *See also* Workouts
  honesty in, 87-88
  for marathons, 53-54, 85-88
  optimization of, 198-199
  pain during, xv, 9
  parameters of, 123-125
  pleasure in, 23-24
  resting as part of, 12, 18-20, 37-46, 51
  specificity of, 128
  for speed, 107-108
  timing in, 12, 14-15
  on tracks, 110
Traveling, running while, 96-98
Triathlete, 178
Triathlon Federation, 177
Triathlons, 127, 176-178
Triathlon Today, 177
True sport, 157
Tutko, Thomas, 157
12-minute test, 121-125
Tymn, Mike, 59-60
Type-A Behavior and Your Heart (Friedman),
  14

U
Ullyot, Joan, 7, 17
Ultrarunning (magazine), 169

V
van Aaken, Ernst, xiv, 31
Viren, Lasse, 181, 186
V̇O₂max. *See* Maximal oxygen uptake

W
Waitz, Grete, 3
Waldron, Meg, 132
Walking
  as cross-training, 30-31
  for distance running, 33-35
  improved performance from, 35-36
  as part of warm-up and cool-down,
    30
  during running. *See* Walking breaks
Walking breaks
  and endurance, 8, 12, 17-18, 31-33, 50,
    145, 191
  timing of, 76-77
Warhol, Michael J., 139
Warm-up
  in interval training, 32
  procedures for, 129-131, 141-143
  walking as part of, 30, 129-131
Water, xv, 191. *See also* Drinking
Weather. *See also* Climate
  changes in, 105-106
  running in cold, 102-105
  running in heat, 101-102, 148
Weidenbach, Lisa, 40
Weight training, 132-133
Welch, Dave, 43
Welch, Jack, 40
Welch, Priscilla, 7, 41, 42-43
Williams, Bob, 219
Williams, Kitty, 169
Williams, Todd, 106, 201-202
Wilt, Fred, xiv, 113, 211
Winning
  versus finishing, 11-12, 13-14
  and personal records, 72
  versus rewards, 153-162
  versus survival, 8-9
Winter, Bud, 223
Wischnia, Bob, 182
Workouts. *See also* Training
  intensity of, 21-23
  pleasure in, 23-24
  simplicity in, 27-28
  surprises in, 25-27
World Association of Veteran Athletes
    (WAVA), 63, 64
Worm-and-turtle stew, 185-186

Y
Young, George, 12, 107-108
Yunxia, Qu, 142-144

Z
Zatopek, Emil, xiv

Books by Joe Henderson

Long, Slow Distance
Road Racers and Their Training
Thoughts on the Run
Run Gently, Run Long
The Long Run Solution
Jog, Run, Race
Run Farther, Run Faster
The Running Revolution
Running, A to Z
Running Your Best Race
Running for Fitness, for Sport and for Life
Joe Henderson's Running Handbook
Total Fitness
Think Fast
Masters Running and Racing (with Bill Rodgers and Priscilla Welch)
Fitness Running (with Richard Brown)
Did I Win?
Better Runs: 25 Years' Worth of Lessons for Running Faster and Farther

About the Author

Joe Henderson has been writing about running for more than 25 years. He's not only the West Coast editor and a featured columnist for *Runner's World* magazine, but also the author of more than a dozen books on running, including *The Long Run Solution*, *Fitness Running*, and *Jog, Run, Race*. He also promotes and participates in running events. As a veteran runner with more than 700 races to his credit, Henderson has seen firsthand how the sport has grown and evolved.

Chuck Palmer

Henderson received his BA from Drake University in 1965. After graduation he worked as an editor in the sports department at the *Des Moines Register* and later as a staff writer for *Track & Field News*. In 1967 he started his long employment with *Runner's World*, where he eventually worked his way up to senior editor. Henderson is also an adjunct assistant professor of journalism at the University of Oregon. In addition, he writes and produces a monthly newsletter called *Running Commentary*.

Henderson is a former executive director of the International Runners Committee, which was instrumental in placing a women's marathon in the Olympics. His honors include being inducted into the Road Runners Club of America Hall of Fame and receiving the club's journalism award in 1979, and being named a Drake University Distinguished Alumnus in 1981. Henderson lives in Eugene, Oregon.